AF797271

APPLICATION SECURITY

A Strategic Roadmap

Y. N. Mahendra

GP
gurucool
PUBLISHING

Published by:

Gurucool Publishing
#102, Sai Krupa Nilayam,
Nagendra Nagar, Habsiguda, Hyderabad - 500007
Ph: 7702566640
E-mail: info@gurucoolpublishing.com

ISBN: 978-93-49999-64-0

First Edition – 2025

For soft copies of the artifacts in this book – email us at **appsecbook.templates@gmail.com** with the serial number of the book.

Gratitude

I, wish to extend my profound gratitude to my parents and family for their unwavering support and encouragement throughout this journey. Their faith in my abilities provided the foundation upon which this work was built.

My sincere thanks go to my dedicated team members, whose invaluable contributions to diagram development, Excel data management, and thorough reference validation links have been instrumental in shaping the quality and precision of this book. Their commitment and expertise are deeply appreciated.

I am also grateful to my peers who generously devoted their time and insight to the technical review process. Their critical feedback and attention to detail enhanced the depth and clarity of the content, ensuring this book meets the highest professional standards.

To all, who played a role in this project, your support has made this endeavour possible.

LEGAL DISCLAIMER

This handbook is for educational purposes and high-level guidance on application security. It is not legal, regulatory, or professional advice, and does not create any consultant-client relationship

The author and publisher of this book have taken due care in the preparation of its content. However, they expressly disclaim any liability for errors, omissions, inaccuracies, discrepancies, or mistakes that may have crept into the publication. Should any such issues be brought to our attention, every effort will be made to address them in subsequent editions. Readers are also advised to refer to the introduction for additional context.

The author is solely responsible for all content presented in this book, including but not limited to views, representations, descriptions, statements, information, opinions, and references. The publisher assumes no responsibility or liability for the same.

Unless otherwise specified, all numerical figures provided in this book are hypothetical, though constructed to resemble realistic values. They are presented solely for illustrative and calculation purposes and should not be construed as actual data.

Any tool names referenced and tool recommendations provided in this book are included exclusively for illustrative and explanatory purposes. Neither the author nor the publisher endorses, promotes, or recommends the purchase or use of any specific tools or products.

The compliance standards and requirements cited herein are not exhaustive or comprehensive. They are presented merely as illustrative examples. Readers are advised to consult the official websites or governing bodies of the respective compliance frameworks for accurate, complete, and up-to-date information.

Similarly, any cost estimates mentioned in this book are solely based on hypothetical numerical assumptions for illustration and demonstration. They should not be treated as actual, reliable, or applicable financial data.

Wherever used, the names of businesses and business owners in the sample asset inventory template are entirely fictitious and provided for illustrative purposes only, and do not refer to any real persons or entities. Any resemblance to real persons, living or dead and/or entities, is purely coincidental.

WARNING: This content is intended for educational purposes only and should be tailored and validated by qualified professionals before implementation. Readers of this book are advised to consult professionals before acting or making a decision. The content mentioned in this book about security guidance, control mappings (e.g., OWASP, ASVS, PCI DSS), and product features change frequently; readers should validate versions and defaults at the time of use. The author and publisher make no representations or warranties, express or implied, regarding the completeness, correctness, or applicability of the information provided in this book. The author and publisher disclaim any liability for direct, indirect, incidental, or consequential damages arising from the use or misuse of the information presented in this book.

All claims and/or disputes arising from or in connection with this publication shall be subject to the exclusive jurisdiction of the competent courts at Hyderabad, India.

Security testing must only be performed with proper authorization and in accordance with applicable laws and contracts.

Accordingly, the reader of this book acknowledges and agrees to the terms of this disclaimer.

The reference links were active and functional during the research, but their current accessibility is uncertain.

Contents

Chapter 1: Introduction

In an era defined by rapid digital transformation, software applications have become the central nervous system of virtually every organization. From intricate enterprise resource planning systems to ubiquitous mobile applications and web services, our reliance on software has never been more profound. These applications facilitate critical business operations, enable global connectivity, drive innovation, and serve as the primary interface between organizations and their customers. This pervasive dependence, brings with it a commensurately expansive and evolving threat landscape. The security of these applications is no longer merely an IT concern, but a fundamental business imperative.

The headlines are replete with stories of devastating **data breaches**, crippling **ransomware attacks**, and the insidious rise of **supply chain compromises**. Each incident underscores a stark reality: vulnerabilities lurking within software applications are frequently the weakest link, serving as direct conduits for malicious actors to access sensitive data, disrupt services, and inflict profound financial and reputational damage. The financial toll of these incidents, coupled with escalating regulatory penalties from mandates like GDPR, HIPAA, and PCI DSS, highlights that neglecting application security is no longer a viable option.

This book serves as a comprehensive guide to building a robust and effective application security program. It is designed for anyone involved in the software development lifecycle – from developers and architects to security professionals, project managers, and business leaders – who recognizes the critical need to embed security into the very fabric of how software is created, deployed, and maintained. Our aim is to demystify application security, providing a pragmatic roadmap for organizations to proactively identify, mitigate, and manage risks throughout the entire software development lifecycle (SDLC).

We will explore the journey of maturing an application security program, moving beyond fragmented, reactive measures to a holistic, integrated, and continuous approach. This involves a fundamental "shift left" in security efforts, pushing security considerations and testing activities as early as possible into the development pipeline. The philosophy underpinning this guide is that security should not be a burdensome gate at the end of development, but a seamless, value-adding component that enables faster, safer innovation.

1.1 Purpose of the Book

The primary purpose of this book is to bridge the gap between theoretical understanding of application security and its practical, actionable implementation within real-world organizations. In a landscape saturated with technical manuals and high-level strategy guides, there remains a critical need for a resource that comprehensively addresses *how* to build, mature, and sustain an effective application security program that aligns with business objectives. This book is crafted to be that definitive resource, offering a pragmatic roadmap for organizations of all sizes and industries.

At its core, this book seeks to equip readers with the knowledge and tools necessary to transform their approach to software security. We aim to move beyond reactive "fix-it-when-it-breaks" mentalities and foster a proactive, "build-security-in" paradigm. This means providing actionable insights into establishing foundational security practices, seamlessly integrating security into agile development workflows, and leveraging advanced automation and intelligence to scale security across vast and complex application portfolios. The goal is not merely to help organizations *avoid* breaches, but to enable them to *innovate* securely, leveraging security as a competitive advantage rather than a costly obligation.

Furthermore, this book emphasizes the crucial interconnectedness of technical security measures with organizational culture and business strategy. It posits that true application security maturity cannot be achieved in isolation by a single security team; rather, it requires a collective commitment, shared responsibility, and consistent collaboration across all departments involved in software delivery. We will delve into how to cultivate a security-aware culture, where every individual involved in the SDLC understands their role in protecting digital assets. By highlighting the tangible business impact of robust security—from significant cost savings to enhanced brand reputation and competitive advantage—the book aims to empower leaders and practitioners alike to justify investments and drive meaningful change. Ultimately, the purpose is to provide a holistic thought that helps organizations build a secure, resilient, and trustworthy digital future.

This quick book intentionally stays at a high level and focuses only on application security strategy and program enablement, (not broader cybersecurity), to help teams kick-start or mature an AppSec program without deep technical detail.

1.2 Why Application Security Testing Matters

The question of "why application security testing matters" has never been more pressing. In the current digital landscape, software applications are the primary conduits for business operations, data exchange, and customer interaction. Consequently, they have become prime targets for cyber attackers, making the security of these applications a critical determinant of an organization's success and survival. Ignoring application security testing is akin to building a magnificent fortress with a glaring, unguarded back door – it renders all other defensive efforts potentially moot.

Firstly, **the escalating cost and frequency of data breaches** serve as a stark reminder. Each year, data breach investigation reports consistently show that the average cost of a data breach is in the millions of dollars, encompassing direct expenses like incident response, legal fees, and regulatory fines, as well as indirect costs such as lost revenue, reputational damage, and customer churn. Many of these breaches originate from vulnerabilities within applications, whether through web applications, APIs, or mobile apps. Application security testing, by proactively identifying and mitigating these weaknesses, directly reduces the likelihood and impact of such catastrophic events. For instance, an organization that invests in SAST and DAST might uncover critical injection flaws that, if left unaddressed, could lead to sensitive data exfiltration and a multi-million-dollar incident.

Secondly, **the pervasive nature of software vulnerabilities** means that security flaws are an inherent part of the development process if not managed effectively. The sheer volume of code, the complexity of modern architectures (microservices, cloud-native, open-source dependencies), and the rapid pace of development cycles all contribute to the potential for vulnerabilities. Application security testing, through methodologies like Software Composition Analysis (SCA), Static Application Security Testing (SAST), and Dynamic Application Security Testing (DAST) weaknesses. Without these tests, organizations are operating with significant "blind spots," unknowingly becoming vulnerable and exposing themselves to exploitation. For example, relying on open-source libraries without SCA is like welcoming unvetted strangers into your home, as known vulnerabilities in these components are frequently exploited.

Thirdly, **regulatory and compliance demands** have tightened considerably, making robust application security a legal obligation, not just a best practice. Regulations such as GDPR, HIPAA, and PCI DSS impose stringent requirements on how organizations handle sensitive data, explicitly mandating secure development practices and regular security assessments. Failure to comply can lead to hefty fines, legal challenges, and restrictions on business operations. Application security testing provides the essential evidence and mechanisms to demonstrate due diligence and adherence to these critical mandates. For instance, conducting annual penetration tests as required by PCI DSS is a direct output of a mature application security testing program.

Fourthly, **the "shift-left" imperative** highlights the immense economic benefits of early vulnerability detection. As illustrated in a chapter, the cost of fixing a security flaw increases exponentially the later it is discovered in the SDLC. A vulnerability found in the design phase might be cheaper to fix, while the same flaw discovered in production could cost thousands or even hundreds of thousands of dollars, not including the potential breach costs. Application security testing, particularly when integrated into developer workflows and CI/CD pipelines, embodies this "shift-left" philosophy, leading to substantial cost savings and accelerated development cycles. Developers receive immediate feedback, allowing to fix issues quickly and efficiently, preventing security from becoming a bottleneck.

Finally, **security as a competitive differentiator** is gaining prominence. In an increasingly security-conscious market, organizations that can credibly demonstrate a superior commitment to data protection and application security gain a significant edge. Customers and partners are more likely to trust and engage with entities that prioritize their security. This translates into enhanced brand reputation, increased customer loyalty, and the ability to win new business, particularly in highly regulated or sensitive sectors. Application security testing provides the objective evidence needed to build this trust and leverage security as a unique selling proposition.

In essence, application security testing is not just about finding bugs; it is a strategic investment that safeguards financial assets, protects reputation, ensures regulatory compliance, accelerates innovation, and builds lasting trust. In a world where software defines business, the security of that software directly defines business resilience.

1.3 Who should read this book

This book is meticulously crafted for a diverse audience, recognizing that effective application security is a shared responsibility that transcends traditional departmental silos. While the technical depth will appeal to practitioners, the strategic insights will be invaluable for leaders making critical business decisions.

1. Software Developers and Engineers: This group forms the bedrock of application security. You are the creators of software, and the security of that software begins with you. This book provides strategies for integrating security tools into your daily development workflows. You will learn how to "shift left" effectively, write inherently more secure code, interpret scan results, and become an active participant in your organization's security posture. Whether you're a frontend, backend, mobile, or full-stack developer, the principles and practices outlined here will empower you to build more resilient applications without sacrificing agility.

2. Software Architects: As the designers of systems, your decisions profoundly impact the security posture of an application before a single line of code is written. This book will update you with methodologies for conducting effective threat modelling, designing secure architectures, selecting secure components, and understanding how different architectural choices introduce or mitigate security risks. You will gain a deeper understanding of how to build security *by design* from the ground up, ensuring that security is baked in, not bolted on.

3. Cybersecurity Professionals (AppSec Engineers, Security Analysts, Penetration Testers): You are the experts on the front lines of defences. This book will help you know the different frameworks available to build and mature an entire application security program. You will learn about selecting, implementing, and orchestrating various security testing tools (SAST, DAST, SCA, IAST, RASP), managing vulnerability backlogs, effectively triaging findings, and leveraging advanced techniques like AI/ML for insights generation. Furthermore, it will guide you on how to become a true enabler for development teams, fostering collaboration, providing actionable guidance, and demonstrating the business value of security.

4. DevSecOps Teams: As the custodians of automated pipelines and production environments, your role in secure delivery is paramount. This book will guide you on integrating security testing seamlessly into CI/CD pipelines, automating security gates, managing secrets securely, and ensuring the secure deployment. You will learn how to build resilient systems that are "secure by default".

5. Project and Product Managers: You are the champions of product vision and delivery timelines. This book will help you understand the critical impact of security on project scope, budget, and release schedules. You will learn how to incorporate security requirements effectively, communicate security risks to stakeholders, and ensure that security is viewed as a value-add that drives customer trust and market differentiation, rather than a project impediment. Your ability to integrate security into product roadmaps is key to sustainable success.

6. C-Suite Executives (CEO, CTO, CIO, CISO) and Business Leaders: Your strategic vision and resource allocation decisions are vital for the success of any application security program. This book will provide you with a clear understanding of the business context of application security, the financial and reputational risks of neglecting it, and the tangible ROI that proactive security initiatives can deliver. You will learn how to define a compelling security vision, set strategic objectives, and interpret key metrics that demonstrate the program's effectiveness and its contribution to the organization's bottom line and competitive advantage.

In essence, this book is for anyone who recognizes that in the digital age, software *is* the business, and securing that software is foundational to sustained success. It is a guide for those who seek to transform application security from a daunting challenge into a strategic strength.

1.4 Structure of the Book

This book is structured to provide a logical progression through the key facets of building, maturing, and measuring an effective application security program. Each chapter builds upon the last, offering a comprehensive and pragmatic roadmap for organizations to navigate the complexities of securing their software assets.

Chapter 1: Introduction (This Chapter) sets the stage by highlighting the critical importance of application security in today's digital landscape. It outlines the purpose of the book, explains why application security testing is indispensable, identifies the diverse audience for whom the book is intended, and provides an overview of the book's structure.

Chapter 2: Business Context delves into the overarching environment that necessitates robust application security. It examines the current security landscape, including the expanding attack surface due to cloud and microservices, and the sophistication of modern threats. The chapter details the scale and cost of data breaches, common application security challenges, and the complex web of regulatory and compliance requirements (like GDPR, HIPAA, PCI DSS). Finally, it discusses the diverse expectations of internal and external stakeholders, emphasizing the need for security to align with business objectives.

Chapter 3: Vision and Ultimate Goal shifts focus to defining the strategic direction for application security. It guides readers through the process of articulating a clear, aspirational security testing vision. The chapter then translates this vision into concrete, measurable long-term objectives across areas of risk reduction, operational efficiency, cultural development, and compliance. A critical element of this chapter is demonstrating how to deeply align security goals with broader business objectives, ensuring that security is seen as an enabler of growth and innovation.

Chapter 4: How Do We Do This? provides the practical, phased roadmap for implementing an application security program. This chapter is divided into three key phases:

- **Phase 1: Foundation** covers establishing security testing basics (SAST, DAST, SCA, manual reviews, pentesting), selecting and implementing the right tools, building a security-aware culture, and conducting initial risk assessments to define baseline metrics.
- **Phase 2: Integration** focuses on embedding security throughout the SDLC. This includes integrating security into planning and design (threat modelling), empowering developers with secure coding practices

and training, and implementing continuous security testing within CI/CD DevSecOps.

- **Phase 3: Automation & Scale** addresses advancing the program through sophisticated automation, leveraging AI and Machine Learning for intelligent threat detection and triage, and scaling security across an entire enterprise application portfolio, including managing legacy applications and supply chain risks. The chapter concludes with the importance of continuous improvement and feedback loops to ensure program adaptability.

Chapter 5: Key Metrics to Measure Success delves into the essential metrics for evaluating the effectiveness and value of the application security program. It provides detailed guidance on tracking:

- **Vulnerability Detection & Remediation Rates:** Quantifying how well vulnerabilities are found and fixed.
- **Mean Time to Detect (MTTD):** Measuring the speed and agility of security operations.
- **Test Coverage & Compliance Adherence:** Ensuring comprehensive security scrutiny and regulatory compliance.
- **ROI of Security Testing Initiatives:** Translating security investments into tangible financial benefits and demonstrating business value.

Chapter 6: Business Impact synthesizes the financial and strategic benefits of a mature application security program. It elaborates on the significant cost savings derived from proactive security (reduced remediation costs, avoided breach expenses, increased operational efficiency, and reduced regulatory fines). The chapter also explores how strong application security enhances brand reputation, builds customer trust, and provides a powerful competitive advantage in the marketplace.

Chapter 7: Conclusion summarizes the key takeaways from the entire book, reinforcing the core principles and benefits of a well-implemented application security program. It outlines crucial next steps for organizations to sustain and continuously mature their security journey. The chapter concludes with a compelling call to action, urging all stakeholders to embrace their role in building a secure digital future where innovation thrives responsibly.

By following this structured approach, readers will gain a comprehensive understanding of how to transform their application security posture, moving from reactive responses to proactive, business-aligned strategies that deliver lasting value.

Chapter 2: Business Context

Before embarking on the journey of building a robust application security program, it is imperative to understand the multifaceted environment in which modern businesses operate. This chapter is dedicated to a critical examination of today's security landscape, the specific challenges organizations commonly face, the non-negotiable regulatory and compliance requirements that govern data handling, and the diverse expectations of key stakeholders. A clear grasp of this context is the bedrock upon which an effective and sustainable application security strategy is built, ensuring that efforts are not just technically sound but also strategically aligned with overarching business goals and realities.

2.1 Overview of the Digital Landscape

The modern business environment is characterized by an unprecedented level of digital reliance. From customer-facing web portals to intricate internal enterprise resource planning (ERP) systems, Management Information Systems (MIS), Customer Relationship Management (CRM) and software applications are the operational backbone of nearly every organization. This pervasive use of technology means that every aspect of operations, customer interactions, and data management is intrinsically linked to the security and integrity of these applications. This widespread dependence has fundamentally reshaped the security landscape, transforming what was once a niche IT concern into a boardroom-level priority.

One of the most significant shifts in recent years is the **rise of remote work and cloud adoption**. The global pivot to telecommuting and flexible work arrangements has dissolved traditional network perimeters. Employees now access sensitive systems from diverse locations and networks, significantly widening the potential attack surface. This necessitates robust endpoint protection, secure VPNs, and, increasingly, the adoption of **Zero Trust Architectures**. The Zero Trust model, which operates on the principle of "never trust, always verify," assumes that threats can exist both inside and outside the network, demanding continuous authentication and strict access controls for all users and devices, regardless of their location. The increase in remote work and cloud adoption puts on top the importance of hardening the applications from security perspective like protecting them from potential attacks on session management, abusing the workflow, and exploit the client-side mechanisms. For organizations, this means re-evaluating traditional perimeter defences and focusing on strengthening the application layer.

Alongside remote work, the accelerated **migration to cloud-native architectures, microservices, and serverless technologies** has further complicated the security equation. While offering immense agility and scalability, these modern architectures introduce new attack vectors. Every new API, container, and microservice expands the attack surface, creating more opportunities for misconfigurations and vulnerabilities. This has led to a burgeoning focus on **API Security**, as Application Programming Interfaces (APIs) have become the connective tissue of modern applications, facilitating interactions between disparate services. Organizations are increasingly realizing that securing these interfaces is paramount, as demonstrated by the surge in API-targeted attacks. For instance, an unpatched API might expose sensitive customer data, leading to a breach even if the core application is otherwise well-secured.

The embrace of **Infrastructure as Code (IaC)**, where infrastructure is provisioned and managed using code, also brings both benefits and security considerations. While IaC promotes consistency and automation, misconfigurations in the code can lead to widespread vulnerabilities if not properly secured and validated. This calls for the integration of security tools that can automatically scan and validate IaC configurations against security best practices.

The evolving nature of cyber threats itself presents a dynamic challenge. Cybercriminals are no longer relying solely on known exploits; they are leveraging advanced technologies, including **AI-based application business logic exploits**. This necessitates equally advanced defensive mechanisms, driving the adoption of **AI-driven security solutions** for real-time threat detection, automated vulnerability assessment, and intelligent incident response. For example, AI can analyse vast amounts of log data, user behaviour, and network traffic to identify anomalies that might indicate a breach, often faster and more accurately than traditional methods.

The application security market itself reflects these trends, with significant growth projected. As of 2025, the market size is estimated at approximately $12.66 billion (**Source:** Coherent Market Insights - "Application Security Market Size, YoY Growth Rate, 2025-2032"), with a projected yearly growth rate of over 14% to reach $18.76 billion by 2028. This growth underscores the increasing investment and recognition of application security as a critical domain.

Finally, there is a profound **cultural shift towards security as a shared responsibility**. The days of security testing being a siloed department are fading. Modern application development demands that security be woven into the fabric of every teams' activities, from developers writing code to operations deploying and monitoring it. Tools and platforms are emerging to foster this collaboration, enabling unified visibility into risks and streamlined communication. For any organization, this means promoting a DevSecOps mindset, where security is an integrated, continuous, and collaborative effort across the entire SDLC, rather than a gate at the end.

In summary, the modern digital landscape is characterized by:

- **Expanded Attack Surface:** Due to remote work, cloud adoption, microservices, and APIs.
- **Sophisticated Threats:** Including AI-driven attacks and persistent zero-day exploits.
- **Shift-Left Imperative:** The need to integrate security early and continuously.
- **Technological Advancements:** Leveraging AI for detection and automation.
- **Cultural Transformation:** Embracing security as a shared, organizational responsibility.

Navigating this complex landscape requires a proactive, strategic, and integrated approach to application security, one that this book aims to help organizations achieve.

2.2 Current Challenges in Application Security

Despite the growing awareness and investment in application security, organizations continue to face significant hurdles. The "shift-left" paradigm, while ideal, is often challenging to implement effectively. The sheer volume and complexity of modern applications, coupled with a relentless and evolving threat landscape, create a dynamic and often overwhelming environment for security teams.

The Scale and Cost of Data Breaches

Data breach statistics paint a stark picture of the consequences of inadequate application security. The average cost of a data breach continues to rise, reaching approximately $4.88 million globally in 2024, a 10% increase from the previous year. For businesses, particularly Small and Medium-sized

Businesses (SMBs) which are less equipped to handle the financial fallout, this burden is particularly heavy. In some industries, like healthcare, the average cost can soar to nearly $10 million due to the highly sensitive nature of patient data.

Key Data Breach Statistics (2023-2025 Trends):

Metric	Statistic	Source (approx.)
Global Average Breach Cost	$4.88 million (2024, 10% increase YoY)	IBM
Healthcare Industry Cost	$9.77 million (average, 2022-2024)	IBM
Breaches involving PII	Nearly 50% involve customer PII	IBM
Breaches involving Cloud	82% of breaches expected to involve cloud-based data (2024)	IBM
Breaches by Human Element	74% of all breaches include the human element	IBM
Time to Identify & Contain	Average 277 days (longer for stolen credentials - 328 days)	IBM, SentinelOne
Unpatched Vulnerabilities	Involved in 60% of data breaches	Research AIMultiple
API Attacks	Over 2 billion blocked by one vendor (2024); targeted 68% more often than websites	Indusface
Supply Chain Attacks	242 publicly reported breaches (2023)	Secureframe
Ransomware Attacks	Increased by 15% in North America (2023), 35% of all attacks globally	SentinelOne

Table 1

These figures underscore the urgent need for robust application security. Attackers are relentless, with reports indicating thousands of cyberattacks occurring daily.

Common Application Security Challenges:

1. **Complexity of Modern Architectures:**
   - **Microservices and APIs:** The decomposition of monolithic applications into smaller, interconnected microservices, often communicating via APIs, creates a highly distributed and complex environment. Each microservice and API endpoint can become a potential attack surface. Managing security across hundreds or thousands of these interconnected components requires sophisticated tooling and processes.
   - **Containerization (Docker, Kubernetes):** While offering portability and efficiency, containers introduce new security concerns related to image vulnerabilities, misconfigurations in container orchestration platforms, and runtime protection.
   - **Cloud Misconfigurations:** Despite the security benefits of cloud providers, misconfigured cloud environments are a leading cause of breaches. This includes misconfigured storage buckets, identity and access management (IAM) policies, and network security groups.
2. **Developer Speed vs. Security:**
   - Modern development cycles are incredibly fast, often driven by Agile and DevOps methodologies. Integrating security without slowing down development is a persistent challenge. Developers are under pressure to deliver features rapidly, and security can sometimes be perceived as a bottleneck or an afterthought.
   - **Lack of Secure Coding Knowledge:** Many developers, while excellent at writing functional code, may lack formal training in secure coding practices. This can lead to the introduction of common vulnerabilities.

- **Tool Integration Friction:** Integrating security tools (SCA,SAST, DAST, IAST) seamlessly into CI/CD pipelines can be complex, requiring significant configuration and maintenance.

3. **Exploding Vulnerability Volume and Alert Fatigue:**

- Over 30,000 new Common Vulnerabilities and Exposures (CVEs) were disclosed in the last year, with half classified as high or critical severity. This sheer volume means security teams are constantly sifting through an overwhelming number of alerts.

- **False Positives:** Many traditional security tools generate a high number of false positives, leading to "alert fatigue" where legitimate threats can be missed amidst the noise. This wastes valuable security team resources and erodes trust in the tools.

4. **Open-Source Software (OSS) and Supply Chain Risks:**

- Modern applications heavily rely on open-source libraries and third-party components. While accelerating development, these components introduce significant supply chain risks if they contain known vulnerabilities. Managing and monitoring these dependencies, often through Software Composition Analysis (SCA) tools, is crucial but challenging at scale. **Example:** The Log4j vulnerability caused widespread panic and remediation efforts across the industry, highlighting the pervasive nature of open-source risks.

5. **The Human Element:**

- Despite technological advancements, human error remains a leading cause of breaches. This includes misconfigurations (21% of error-related breaches), mistaken delivery of sensitive information (43%), and publishing errors (23%).

- **Insider Threats:** Whether malicious or negligent, insiders pose a significant risk. For instance, 12% of employees in one study took sensitive IP with them when they left an organization. Negligent or mistaken insiders account for 55% of insider incidents, while malicious insiders make up 25%.
- **Phishing and Social Engineering:** These attacks continue to be highly effective, often serving as the initial entry point for more sophisticated attacks.

6. **Emerging Threats from Generative AI (GenAI):**
   - While GenAI can assist developers, code generated by AI is not inherently secure and can introduce new vulnerabilities if not rigorously tested. Research has revealed "critical security blindspots" associated with AI-generated code and its use of third-party open-source software. Organizations must apply the same, if not more, scrutiny to AI-generated code as they do to human-written code.
7. **Talent Shortage and Skill Gaps:**
   - There is a persistent global shortage of skilled cybersecurity professionals, particularly in the specialized field of application security. This makes it difficult for organizations to build and staff effective AppSec teams, leading to overworked personnel and unaddressed risks.

These challenges highlight the complexity and dynamism of application security. Successfully navigating them requires not just tools, but a strategic approach that integrates people, processes, and technology, fostering a culture of continuous security improvement.

2.3 Regulatory and Compliance Requirements

In an increasingly regulated global economy, robust application security is not just a best practice; it's a legal and ethical imperative. A growing labyrinth of national and international regulations, coupled with industry-specific standards, mandates how organizations collect, process, store, and transmit sensitive data. Non-compliance carries severe consequences, including substantial financial penalties, legal action, reputational damage, and loss of business licenses. For any organization, understanding and adhering to these requirements is critical for maintaining operational integrity and market trust.

The intersection of regulatory compliance and application security means that security controls must be built directly into the applications themselves, not merely layered on top. This "security by design" principle is increasingly a foundational element of compliance.

Here are some of the most prominent regulatory and compliance requirements impacting application security:

1. General Data Protection Regulation (GDPR)

- **Scope:** A landmark data privacy and security law in the European Union (EU) that also applies globally to organizations that collect, process, or store personal data of EU residents.
- **Key Application Security Implications:**
  - **Data Protection by Design and by Default (Article 25):** Mandates that data protection and privacy considerations are integrated into the design and implementation of applications from the very beginning. This means building security features like encryption, pseudonymization, and access controls into the application architecture.
  - **Security of Processing (Article 32):** Requires organizations to implement appropriate technical and organizational measures to ensure a level of security appropriate to the risk. This includes regular testing,

assessing, and evaluating the effectiveness of security measures (e.g., vulnerability scanning, penetration testing).

- **Data Minimization:** Applications should only collect and process personal data that is necessary for a specific purpose.
- **Individual Rights:** Applications must support data subjects' rights, such as the right to access their data, rectify inaccuracies, request erasure ("right to be forgotten"), and object to processing.
- **Breach Notification:** Organizations must notify the relevant supervisory authority of a data breach within 72 hours of becoming aware of it, and potentially individuals if the breach poses a high risk to their rights and freedoms.

- **Penalties:** Up to €20 million or 4% of annual global turnover, whichever is higher.

2. Health Insurance Portability and Accountability Act (HIPAA)

- **Scope:** A U.S. federal law establishing national standards to protect sensitive patient health information (PHI). Applies to healthcare providers, health plans, healthcare clearinghouses, and their business associates.
- **Key Application Security Implications:**
- **Security Rule:** Requires administrative, physical, and technical safeguards to ensure the confidentiality, integrity, and availability of Electronic Protected Health Information (ePHI). For applications, this translates to:
- **Access Controls:** Restricting access to ePHI to authorized personnel and software components.
- **Encryption:** Encrypting ePHI both at rest and in transit.

- **Audit Controls:** Implementing mechanisms to record and examine activity in information systems that contain or use ePHI.
- **Integrity Controls:** Protecting ePHI from improper alteration or destruction.
- **Authentication:** Verifying that a person or entity seeking access to ePHI is the one claimed.

- **Privacy Rule:** Protects the privacy of PHI, including how it is used and disclosed.
- **Breach Notification Rule:** Requires covered entities and business associates to notify affected individuals, the Department of Health and Human Services (HHS), and in some cases, the media, following a breach of unsecured PHI.
  - **Common Violations:** Often involve unsecured methods of sharing PHI, weak third-party technologies, and improper disposal of ePHI, all of which can be prevented by robust application security.

3. Payment Card Industry Data Security Standard (PCI DSS)

  - **Scope:** A set of security standards designed to ensure that all companies that process, store, or transmit credit card information maintain a secure environment. It is mandated by the major credit card brands.

- **Key Application Security Implications (PCI DSS v4.0.1):**
  - **Requirement 6 (Secure Systems and Software):** This is highly relevant to AppSec. It mandates that all web-facing applications are protected from known attacks, addressing vulnerabilities like injection flaws, buffer overflows, and insecure cryptographic storage.

  - **Web Application Firewalls (WAFs):** PCI DSS 4.0.1 (effective March 31, 2025) requires organizations to implement WAFs for public-facing web applications to detect and block attacks.

- **Secure Coding Practices:** Developers must be trained in secure coding techniques, and code reviews must incorporate security.
- **Vulnerability Management Program:** Regular security testing (vulnerability scans, penetration tests) of applications and networks handling cardholder data.
- **Tamper-Detection:** Requirement 11.6.1 requires tamper-detection mechanisms on payment pages to detect and address any unauthorized changes.
- **Strict Access Controls:** Limiting access to cardholder data based on business need-to-know.

4. Sarbanes-Oxley Act (SOX)

- **Scope:** A U.S. federal law enacted to protect investors from fraudulent accounting activities by corporations. While not a direct security law, its sections (especially 302, 404, 906) indirectly impact IT and application security.
- **Key Application Security Implications:**
  - **Internal Controls:** SOX requires public companies to establish and maintain internal controls over financial reporting. Since applications process and store financial data, their security, integrity, and availability are crucial to SOX compliance.
  - **Data Accuracy and Security:** Applications must ensure the accuracy and security of financial data, which implies strong access controls, audit trails, and protection against manipulation or unauthorized access.
  - **Cloud Computing:** When financial data is stored and processed in the cloud, SOX extends to cloud computing, requiring organizations to implement controls like encryption and access control for cloud-based financial data.

5. Other Notable Regulations and Standards

- **California Consumer Privacy Act (CCPA) / California Privacy Rights Act (CPRA):** U.S. state-level laws providing California consumers with robust data privacy rights, similar in spirit to GDPR, including rights to know, delete, and opt-out of the sale of personal information. This necessitates secure data handling in applications.
- **India's Digital Personal Data Protection Act (DPDP Act):** India's comprehensive data privacy law, similar to GDPR, focusing on consent, data minimization, and individual rights. Will require significant application security measures for companies handling Indian citizens' data.
- **ISO/IEC 27001:** An international standard for Information Security Management Systems (ISMS). While not a law, compliance with ISO 27001 demonstrates a systematic approach to managing information security risks, including application security. It emphasizes security integration into software development, security testing, and vulnerability management.
- **NIST (National Institute of Standards and Technology):** NIST provides a comprehensive framework for improving cybersecurity across industries. Its Cybersecurity Framework (CSF) helps organizations identify, protect, detect, respond, and recover from cyber threats. It offers guidelines on risk management, continuous monitoring, and security practices, crucial for protecting critical infrastructure. NIST's standards and publications are widely adopted in both the government and private sectors.
- **CSA (Cloud Security Alliance):** The CSA is a leading organization focused on cloud computing security. It provides best practices and guidelines through frameworks such as the Cloud Controls Matrix (CCM) and Security, Trust & Assurance Registry (STAR). These frameworks help organizations ensure that their cloud services meet industry security standards and protect sensitive data. CSA

also works on advancing cloud security research and promoting secure cloud adoption practices.

- **SOC 2 (Service Organization Control Type 2):** A reporting framework for service organizations that specifies how they should protect customer data. Relevant for SaaS providers and other service organizations, focusing on security, availability, processing integrity, confidentiality, and privacy.

Summary of Key Compliance Requirements for Application Security

Regulation / Standard	Primary Focus	Key AppSec Implications	Example Control/Practice
GDPR	Personal Data Privacy	Data Protection by Design: Secure storage, processing, and transmission of personal data; data minimization. Breach Notification	Data protection impact assessments (DPIA), Access Control, Encrypting personal data at rest and in transit
HIPAA	Health Information (PHI)	Ensure confidentiality, integrity, and availability of electronic PHI (ePHI); audit controls; transmission security	Role-based access control to patient records, audit logging, secure messaging systems, encryption at rest and in transit
PCI DSS	Cardholder Data	Secure Systems, network & Software, WAF, Vulnerability Management, RBAC	Regular web app penetration tests, WAF deployment, file integrity monitoring, MFA,
SOX	Financial transparency	Ensure the integrity and	Strong authentication for

	and reporting accuracy	security of financial data; auditability of financial systems	financial applications, Change management controls, logging and monitoring of access to financial records, and automated audit trails
ISO 27001	Information Security ISMS	Establish systematic management of sensitive information; implement risk management Integrated Security, Security Testing in SDLC, Vuln Management	Risk assessment procedures, security policy enforcement, employee training, continual monitoring and improvement, Secure coding guidelines for developers

Table 2

The common thread across these regulations is the demand for a proactive, integrated, and continuously assessed approach to security within applications. For organizations, achieving and maintaining compliance means embedding application security into every phase of the SDLC, regularly auditing practices, and staying abreast of evolving legal landscapes.

2.4 Stakeholder Expectations

An effective application security program is not just a technical endeavour; it's a cross-functional initiative that impacts and is impacted by various stakeholders across the organization and beyond. Understanding and managing the diverse expectations of these groups is crucial for gaining buy-in, securing resources, and ensuring the success and sustainability of security initiatives. Failure to address these expectations can lead to resistance, misunderstandings, and ultimately, program failure.

Stakeholders in application security typically fall into internal and external categories:

Internal Stakeholders:

1. **C-Suite Executives (CEO, CTO, CIO, CISO):**
   - **Expectations:** Primarily concerned with the **business impact** of security. They expect the application security program to reduce organizational risk (e.g., data breaches, regulatory fines), protect brand reputation, ensure business continuity, and potentially provide a competitive advantage. They seek clear **ROI (Return on Investment)** on security spend, concise reporting on risk posture, and assurance that compliance requirements are met without impeding innovation or market agility. They need strategic insights, not just technical jargon.

Example: The CEO expects to see a measurable reduction in critical vulnerabilities over time, translating to lower potential financial liabilities and enhanced market trust. The CISO expects to effectively communicate risk to the board and demonstrate continuous improvement in the security posture, showing the risk reduction.

2. **Board of Directors:**
   - **Expectations:** The Board is responsible for governance and strategic oversight, holding the C-Suite accountable for risk management. They expect high-level, non-technical reporting on the company's overall cybersecurity risk posture and its potential impact on enterprise value and long-term strategy. Their concerns revolve around fiduciary duty, brand reputation, and regulatory compliance. They expect assurance that the application security program is adequately resourced and aligned with business goals to protect shareholder value.

Example: At a quarterly risk committee meeting, a director might question the CISO on the company's exposure to a recent zero-day vulnerability, asking for a clear, concise assessment of the financial and reputational risk, and a high-level plan for remediation, rather than the technical details of the fix.

3. **Development Teams (Developers, Engineers, Architects):**
   - **Expectations:** They want security processes and tools that are **easy to integrate** into their existing workflows and do not significantly hinder productivity. They expect accurate and **actionable security findings** (minimal false positives), clear guidance on how to remediate vulnerabilities, and access to secure coding training. They value tools that provide fast feedback loops, allowing them to fix issues early in the development cycle. They also appreciate frameworks and libraries that are secure by default, simplifying their task.

Example: A developer expects their IDE to highlight security flaws as they type code, or for a static analysis tool in the CI/CD pipeline to provide specific line numbers and remediation advice for detected vulnerabilities specific to that context, rather than just a generic error message.

4. **DevSecOps Teams:**
   - **Expectations:** They seek security solutions that support **automation and continuous delivery**. They expect security tools to be stable, scalable, and integrate seamlessly into CI/CD pipelines without introducing significant friction or downtime. Their focus is on ensuring the secure deployment and reliable operation of applications in production environments.

Example: A DevOps engineer expects security scans to run automatically as part of the build process, flagging critical issues before deployment, and for security configurations to be managed as code alongside application infrastructure.

5. **Quality Assurance (QA) and Testing Professionals:**
   - **Expectations:** While their primary focus is functional quality, they increasingly expect to incorporate **security testing into their existing test cycles**. They look for clear test cases, methodologies, and tools that help them identify security flaws alongside functional bugs. They expect security test results to be integrated into their defect tracking systems.

Example: A QA tester might use a dynamic application security testing (DAST) tool or tools like Cross Site Scripting (XSS) Finder and Insecure Direct Object Reference (IDOR) Detectors as part of their testing suite to identify runtime vulnerabilities, with findings appearing in the same bug tracking system used for functional defects.

6. **Project and Product Managers:**
   - **Expectations:** They need to understand the **impact of security on project timelines, budgets, and feature roadmaps**. They expect clear communication of security risks, priorities, and progress. They want to ensure security requirements are properly scoped and resourced, and that security efforts align with product release cycles and market demands.

Example: A product manager needs to know if a critical security vulnerability will delay a product launch, how much it will cost to fix, and how the fix will be communicated to customers.

7. **Legal and Compliance Teams:**
   - **Expectations:** They are focused on **regulatory adherence and legal risk mitigation**. They expect the application security program to demonstrate due diligence, provide audit trails, and ensure that applications comply with all

applicable laws and standards (GDPR, HIPAA, PCI DSS, etc.). They require clear documentation of security policies, procedures, and controls.

Example: The compliance officer requires documented evidence that all applications processing sensitive customer data undergo regular security assessments to meet GDPR's "security by design" requirements.

External Stakeholders:

1. **Customers and End-Users:**

- **Expectations:** Primarily concerned with the **privacy and security of their data**, and the **reliability and trustworthiness** of the applications they use. They expect their personal information to be protected, and services to be consistently available and free from security incidents. A breach can severely erode their trust and lead to abandonment of services.

Example: A user of a mobile banking app expects their financial transactions to be secure, their account information to be protected, and the app to be available whenever they need it, without fear of their data being compromised.

2. **Regulatory Authorities:**

- **Expectations:** They expect **strict adherence to laws and standards** to protect consumer data and ensure market integrity. They require transparent reporting of breaches, demonstrable evidence of security controls, and often mandate specific security measures for applications operating within their jurisdiction.

Example: A data protection authority might investigate a company after a reported breach, demanding evidence of application security measures and compliance with GDPR.

3. **Partners and Suppliers:**
   - **Expectations:** They expect that any applications or systems they integrate with are secure, and that their own data (and that of their shared customers) is protected. They require assurances of the organization's security posture and often conduct security assessments or demand specific security certifications.

Example: A payment gateway provider expects the e-commerce platform they integrate with to be PCI DSS compliant, ensuring secure handling of cardholder data throughout the transaction process.

4. **Investors and Shareholders:**
   - **Expectations:** They are interested in the **financial health and long-term viability** of the company. Security failures can directly impact stock prices, investor confidence, and market valuation. They expect management to have a robust strategy for managing cyber risks, including application security.

Effectively managing these diverse expectations requires constant communication, transparency, and a clear understanding of each group's priorities. By aligning application security efforts with the strategic objectives of all stakeholders, organizations can build a security program that not only protects digital assets but also fuels business growth and fosters lasting trust. This holistic view ensures that security is seen not as a separate entity, but as an integral part of how any organization delivers value to its customers and stakeholders.

Chapter 3: Vision and Ultimate Goal

Having established the current business context, the prevailing security landscape, and the challenges organizations face in Chapter 2, it's time to cast our gaze forward. This chapter is dedicated to defining the aspirational future state for application security within any organization. It's about articulating a clear vision, setting ambitious yet achievable long-term objectives, and critically, ensuring that these security goals are deeply intertwined with, and actively support, the broader business objectives of the organization. Without a well-defined vision and strategic alignment, security initiatives can become fragmented, reactive, and ultimately fail to deliver meaningful value.

3.1 Defining the Security Testing Vision

A security testing vision is more than just a statement of intent; it is a concise, inspiring, and forward-looking declaration that articulates the desired future state of application security within an organization. It serves as a guiding star, providing direction, purpose, and a shared understanding for all stakeholders involved. For any organization, defining this vision is a foundational step, as it sets the strategic tone for all subsequent activities and investments in application security.

What is a Security Testing Vision?

At its core, a security testing vision describes what success looks like for application security in the long run. It answers the fundamental question: "Where do we want to be with our application security efforts in X years?" This vision should be:

- Aspirational and Inspiring: It should motivate teams and individuals to strive for excellence, painting a picture of a more secure, resilient, and trusted future.
- Clear and Concise: Easily understood by technical and non-technical stakeholders alike. It avoids overly technical jargon and focuses on the high-level impact.
- Strategic: It transcends mere technical implementation, connecting security outcomes to business value and organizational objectives.
- Stable yet Flexible: While the vision itself should be relatively enduring, the roadmap to achieve it can evolve based on changing threats, technologies, and business priorities.
- Collaboratively Developed: To foster ownership and buy-in, the vision should not be dictated top-down but crafted with input from various departments, including development, operations, business leadership, legal, and security.

Why is a Clear Vision Important?

Defining a clear vision for application security offers several critical benefits for an organization:

1. Provides Direction and Focus: In a complex domain like cybersecurity, it's easy to get lost in the weeds of specific vulnerabilities or tools. A clear vision ensures that all efforts, from individual coding practices to enterprise-wide tool deployments, are aligned towards a common, comprehensive goal. It prevents reactive security efforts and promotes a proactive, strategic approach.
1. Facilitates Resource Allocation: When the vision is clear and tied to business outcomes, it becomes significantly easier to justify investments in application security. Leaders can understand *why* certain tools, training, or personnel are needed, making resource allocation decisions more straightforward and effective.

2. Fosters Cultural Shift and Buy-in: Security is a shared responsibility. A compelling vision helps communicate *why* every developer, tester, and business unit needs to care about application security. It moves security from being perceived as a barrier to being a shared objective for delivering higher-quality software and services. For example, if the vision emphasizes "quick and frictionless secure development," developers are more likely to embrace new security tools that support this goal.
3. Enables Measurement of Progress: A clear vision provides the ultimate benchmark against which progress can be measured. While specific metrics will track short-term objectives, the vision provides the north star to assess if the overall traction is correct.
4. Adapts to Evolving Threats: Even as the threat landscape shifts, a strong vision helps guide how the organization adapts its security strategy. It encourages continuous improvement and resilience rather than just responding to the latest threats.

Process of Defining the Vision for an Organization:

The journey to defining an organization's security testing vision should involve several key steps:

1. Assess the Current State: Before defining the future, understand the present. This involves reviewing existing application security maturity (tools, processes, people, culture), identifying current pain points (e.g., late-stage vulnerability discovery, frequent breaches), and understanding the impact of these issues on the business.
2. Identify Key Stakeholders and Their Perspectives: Engage leadership, development teams, operations, legal, risk, and business units. Understand their concerns, priorities, and aspirations related to application security. This collaborative input is vital for crafting a vision that resonates across the organization.

3. Brainstorm Core Tenets: Based on the assessment and stakeholder input, identify the core principles and values that will underpin the organization's approach to application security. These might include "security by design," "developer enablement," "continuous assurance," or "risk-based prioritization."
4. Draft Initial Vision Statements: Develop several potential vision statements. These should be concise and impactful.
    - *Initial Draft Example 1 (Too Technical):* "Implement SAST, DAST, and SCA in all CI/CD pipelines to find all vulnerabilities." (Lacks inspiration and strategic focus).
    - *Initial Draft Example 2 (Better, but not specific enough):* "Be a leader in cybersecurity." (Too vague, doesn't specify *how* or *what* aspects).
5. Refine and Articulate the Vision: Select the most compelling statement and refine it. Ensure it is:
    - Concise: One or two sentences.
    - Memorable: Easy to recall and repeat.
    - Inspirational: Creates a sense of purpose.
    - Future-Oriented: Describes the desired end state.
    - Business-Aligned: Connects to broader organizational success.

Example Vision Statement for an Organization: "To foster a pervasive culture of secure software development that proactively embeds security into every layer of our applications, protecting our customers, safeguarding our data, and fuelling business innovation with unwavering trust and resilience."

This vision emphasizes culture, proactive measures, customer protection, data security, innovation, trust, and resilience – all critical elements for any modern organization. It's not just about finding vulnerabilities; it's about building security inherently into the entire software ecosystem and leveraging it as a business differentiator.

3.2 Long-Term Objectives for the Organization

Once the overarching vision is defined, the next crucial step is to translate that vision into concrete, measurable, and time-bound long-term objectives. These objectives serve as milestones on the journey towards achieving the vision, providing specific targets that allow the organization to track progress, allocate resources strategically, and hold teams accountable. Unlike day-to-day tasks, long-term objectives typically span several years and require sustained effort across multiple initiatives.

When setting these objectives, it's beneficial to use the SMART (Specific, Measurable, Achievable, Relevant, and Time-Bound) criteria or OKR's:

- Specific: Clearly defined, not vague.
- Measurable: Quantifiable, so progress can be tracked.
- Achievable: Realistic given resources and constraints.
- Relevant: Aligned with the vision and business goals.
- Time-bound: Has a defined timeframe for achievement.

For an organization, long-term application security objectives might span several key areas:

1. Risk Reduction Objectives

These objectives focus on quantitatively decreasing the organization's exposure to application-related security risks.

- Objective Example: Reduce the average number of critical and high-severity vulnerabilities in production applications by 75% (from the baseline security assessment) within the next three years.

- *Rationale:* Directly addresses the threat landscape and potential for breaches. Measures the effectiveness of "shift-left" and "security testing" practices.
- *Measurement:* Track vulnerability density per application, severity distribution, and number of vulnerabilities reaching production.

- Objective Example: Decrease the Mean Time to Remediate (MTTR) critical and high-severity application vulnerabilities from X days to Y days (e.g., 90 days to 15 days) across all new development by the end of year 2.
  - *Rationale:* Focuses on the efficiency of the remediation process, reducing the window of exposure.
  - *Measurement:* Calculate the average time from vulnerability discovery to fix deployment.

2. Operational Efficiency and Automation Objectives

These objectives aim to streamline security processes, reduce manual effort, and improve the speed at which security checks are performed.

- Objective Example: Automate 80% of routine application security testing activities (e.g., Secrets scanning, SCA, SAST scans, basic DAST checks) within CI/CD pipelines for all major applications within 24 months.
  - *Rationale:* Addresses developer speed vs. security challenge, frees up security team for more complex tasks, and ensures consistent security checks.
  - *Measurement:* Percentage of pipelines with integrated automated scans, reduction in manual security review hours.

- Objective Example: Implement an integrated Application Security Posture Management (ASPM) platform or proprietary dashboard to provide a unified view of application security risks and remediation status across the enterprise within 18 months.
    - *Rationale:* Solves alert fatigue and provides centralized visibility, enabling better decision-making and resource prioritization.
    - *Measurement:* Deployment status of the platform, adoption rate among teams, reduction in time spent aggregating security data from disparate sources.

3. Cultural and Capability Development Objectives

These objectives focus on building a strong security-aware culture and enhancing the skills of development teams.

- Objective Example: Achieve a 90% completion rate for mandatory secure coding training among all software developers and architects by the end of the first year.
    - *Rationale:* Directly addresses the "lack of secure coding knowledge" challenge, embedding security into developer practices.
    - *Measurement:* Training completion rates, pre/post-training knowledge assessments.
- Objective Example: Establish a dedicated internal AppSec Champions program, identifying and training at least one security champion in every major development team within 12 months.
    - *Rationale:* Promotes security as a shared responsibility, provides in-team security expertise, and scales security knowledge horizontally.
    - *Measurement:* Number of identified and trained champions, documented activities of champions.

4. Compliance and Governance Objectives

These objectives ensure that the organization meets its legal and regulatory obligations and maintains a strong governance framework.

- Objective Example: Ensure 100% of applications handling sensitive customer data (e.g., PII, PHI, cardholder data) undergo annual independent security assessments (e.g., penetration tests) to satisfy compliance and regulatory requirements within the next two years.
  - *Rationale:* Directly addresses compliance mandates like GDPR, HIPAA, and PCI DSS.
  - *Measurement:* Number/percentage of applications assessed, audit findings related to compliance.
- Objective Example: Develop and enforce clear, documented application security policies and secure coding guidelines for all new development initiatives within 12 months.
  - *Rationale:* Provides a consistent framework for secure development, essential for governance and compliance.
  - *Measurement:* Policy approval and dissemination, adherence rate (e.g., via automated checks).

5. Innovation and Business Enablement Objectives

These objectives highlight how security can accelerate, rather than impede, business agility and market advantage.

- Objective Example: Reduce security-related delays in critical application release cycles by 50% within the next two years through integrated security testing and automated gates.
  - *Rationale:* Positions security as an enabler of speed to market.
  - *Measurement:* Track average security review/remediation time per release, number of releases delayed due to security issues.
- Objective Example: Enhance customer trust and improve customer satisfaction scores related to data security by 10%

within the next three years, leveraging secure product features and transparent security communications.

- *Rationale:* Directly links security to brand reputation and customer loyalty.
- *Measurement:* Customer satisfaction surveys, public perception analysis, reduction in security-related SIEM events and customer complaints.

These long-term objectives provide a structured approach for any organization to operationalize its application security vision, ensuring that efforts are focused, measurable, and aligned with strategic priorities. Each objective will then be broken down into smaller, actionable initiatives and projects, as detailed in later chapters on the roadmap.

Sample OKR Sheet - Table 3

Objective #	Focus Area	Description	Target Date	Progress (%)	Status	Comments
1	**Risk Reduction**	Reduce the average number of critical and high-severity vulnerabilities				
	Key Result 1	Reduce the average number of critical and high-severity vulnerabilities in production applications by 75% within the next three years.	<<Date>>	%	In-progress	
	Key Result 2	Decrease the Mean Time to Remediate (MTTR) critical and high-severity application vulnerabilities from X days to Y days (e.g., 90 days to 15 days) across all new development by end of year 2.	<<Date>>	%	In-progress	
2	**Automation**	Streamline security processes, reduce manual effort, and improve the speed at which security checks are performed.				
	Key Result 1	Automate 80% of routine application security testing activities (e.g., Secrets scanning, SCA, SAST scans, basic DAST checks) within CI/CD pipelines for all major applications within 24 months.	<<Date>>	%	To start	
3	**Culture**	Build a strong security-aware culture and enhancing the skills of development teams.				
	Key Result 1	Achieve a 90% completion rate for mandatory secure coding training among all software developers and architects by the end of the first year.	<<Date>>	%	To start	

3.3 Aligning Security with Business Goals

The most critical aspect of any successful application security program is its deep and unwavering alignment with the comprehensive business goals of the organization. For too long, security has been viewed as a cost centre, a necessary evil, or a roadblock to innovation. This perception often leads to underinvestment, friction between teams, and reactive security postures. To truly thrive, application security within an organization must transform from a perceived impediment into a recognized business enabler and a source of competitive advantage.

Aligning security with business goals means speaking the language of the business: risk, revenue, reputation, customer trust, market share, and operational efficiency. It's about demonstrating how a secure application directly contributes to these objectives.

Why Alignment is Crucial:

1. Securing Resources and Budget: When security initiatives clearly support business objectives, it becomes easier to gain executive buy-in and secure the necessary financial and human resources. Business leaders are more likely to invest when they understand the direct return on that investment.

2. Driving Adoption and Buy-in: If development teams understand that security helps them deliver higher-quality, more resilient products that customers trust (a business goal), they are more likely to embrace secure coding practices and security tools.

3. Prioritizing Efforts: Not all vulnerabilities or security initiatives have the same business impact. Alignment helps prioritize security efforts based on their potential impact on

critical business functions, revenue streams, or compliance obligations.

4. Enabling Innovation and Agility: When security is embedded into the development process from the start, it /prevents late-stage security bottlenecks. Developers can innovate faster, knowing that security checks are automated and proactive, leading to quicker, more secure product releases.

5. Building Customer Trust and Brand Reputation: In a competitive market, security can be a differentiator. Customers are increasingly aware of data privacy and security. A demonstrable commitment to application security builds trust, enhances brand reputation, and can attract and retain customers.

Strategies for Achieving Alignment:

1. Understand the Business: Security professionals must move beyond technical details and genuinely understand the organization's business model, revenue streams, critical operations, and strategic initiatives. What applications are most critical for revenue? Which data is most sensitive? What new markets is the organization entering?
2. Speak the Business Language: Translate security risks and benefits into terms that resonate with business leaders. Instead of saying "We need to fix XSS vulnerabilities," say "Addressing XSS flaws will prevent potential customer data theft, protect our brand reputation, and avoid millions in potential breach costs."

- From Technical Term to Business Impact:
    - "SQL Injection vulnerability" → "Risk of sensitive customer database compromise, leading to data theft and regulatory fines."

  - "Lack of DAST in pre-production" → "Blind spots to runtime vulnerabilities that could result in service downtime and loss of customer trust."
  - "High volume of open-source vulnerabilities" → "Increased exposure to supply chain attacks, potentially compromising intellectual property or leading to widespread system outages."

3. Involve Business Leaders Early and Continuously: Security should be a standing item in business strategy discussions, not just an IT meeting. Involve C-level executives, product managers, and legal teams in defining the application security vision and objectives. Their perspectives are crucial for prioritization and resource allocation.

4. Integrate Security into Product Development Cycles: Instead of being a separate "security phase," application security must be woven into every stage of the product lifecycle, from ideation and requirements gathering to design, development, testing, deployment, and operations.
   - **Example**: When a new feature is proposed, security architects should be involved in impact analysis and threat modelling discussions from the outset, identifying potential risks and designing secure controls *before* a line of code is written.
5. Demonstrate Return on Investment (ROI): Quantify the benefits of security investments. This can be challenging, but it is vital.
   - Cost Savings: Show how early detection and remediation of vulnerabilities reduce the cost of fixing bugs later (e.g., "A critical bug found in design costs $100 to fix, but $10,000 in production").
   - Reduced Risk: Use metrics like reduction in critical vulnerabilities, risk exposure reduction, or avoided compliance fines.

- Enhanced Reputation: Link security improvements to positive customer feedback, brand perception surveys, or competitive differentiation.
- Market Enablement: Show how robust security enables entry into new, highly regulated markets or allows for more secure digital services.

6. Develop a Risk-Based Approach: Prioritize security efforts based on the actual business risk posed by applications and their data. A public-facing e-commerce application handling payment data will require more stringent security measures than an internal static documentation portal. This ensures that the most critical assets receive the most attention.

Table: Aligning Application Security with Business Goals

The table 4 - below illustrates how common business goals directly benefit from a strong application security program.

Business Goal	How Application Security Contributes	Example Metric to Track
Increase Customer Trust & Loyalty	Proactive security measures protect customer data and privacy, reducing the likelihood of breaches. Transparent communication about security practices builds confidence. Secure applications offer a reliable and safe user experience.	Number of Security Incidents Involving Customer Data, Customer Churn Rate (security-related), User Engagement with Security Features, Net Promoter Score (security dimension).

Protect Brand Reputation	Avoiding costly and embarrassing data breaches prevents negative media coverage and public outcry. Demonstrating a commitment to security leadership and responsible data handling enhances public image.	Brand sentiment score (positive vs. negative mentions), Media coverage analysis (volume, tone, reach), Social media engagement (negative comments, crisis-related volume), Cost of breach (including recovery, fines, legal fees, lost business).
Achieve Regulatory Compliance	Implementing security controls by design ensures adherence to data privacy laws (GDPR, HIPAA, CCPA) and industry standards (PCI DSS). Regular audits and documented processes provide evidence of compliance, avoiding fines and legal action.	Audit findings, compliance reports, reduction in legal fees/fines.
Accelerate Time-to-Market / Innovation	Embedding security into the SDLC ("Shift Left") ensures vulnerabilities are identified and fixed	Average time from code commit to production release, number

	early, preventing costly and time-consuming rework before release. Automation of security checks reduces friction and speeds up delivery pipelines.	of security-related release delays.
Reduce Operational Costs	Fixing vulnerabilities early in development is significantly cheaper than post-deployment fixes or responding to an active breach. Automation reduces manual security effort. Prevention of breaches avoids cleanup, legal, and reputational costs.	Cost of fixing vulnerabilities at different SDLC stages, avoided breach costs, and security testing team efficiency.
Gain Competitive Advantage	Offering demonstrably more secure products than competitors can attract privacy-conscious customers. Compliance with stringent regulations allows easy entry into new markets or partnerships that require high security standards.	Market share in security-sensitive sectors, successful security assessments by partners, and customer testimonials.
Ensure Business Continuity	Secure applications are more resilient to attacks, reducing the risk of downtime, service disruptions, and data loss. Robust incident response	System Uptime percentage, Number of downtime incidents, Average time to restore service

	capabilities minimize the impact of any successful attacks, allowing for quicker recovery.	after a security incident.

Table 4

By actively pursuing these alignment strategies, any organization can transform its application security program from a defensive necessity into a strategic asset that not only protects the organization but also directly contributes to its growth, profitability, and standing in the market. This holistic view ensures that security is seen not as a separate entity, but as an integral part of how an organization delivers value to its customers and stakeholders.

Chapter 4: How Do We Do This?

Having established a clear vision and long-term objectives for application security, the fundamental question arises: *How do we actually achieve this?* This chapter provides a pragmatic, phased roadmap for building, integrating, and scaling an effective application security program within any organization. It acknowledges that transforming security practices is not an overnight task but a continuous journey requiring strategic planning, incremental implementation, and a commitment to cultural change. We will break down this journey into three distinct phases: establishing a foundational bedrock, seamlessly integrating security into daily development workflows, and finally, automating and scaling security to an enterprise level while fostering continuous improvement.

Phase 1: Foundation

The initial phase is about establishing the non-negotiable groundwork for application security. It focuses on setting up the basic capabilities, selecting the right initial tools, cultivating a security-aware mindset, and performing essential assessments to understand the starting point. Without a solid foundation, subsequent efforts will likely crumble under the weight of complexity and unmet expectations.

4.1 Establishing Security Testing Basics

Before delving into advanced techniques, an organization must grasp and implement the fundamental types of security testing. These basics form the core techniques for identifying vulnerabilities in software. It's crucial to start simple, focusing on the most impactful methods, and then gradually expand coverage and sophistication.

Identifying the requirements to start security testing

Sl. No	1	2	3
Application Name	App 1	App 2	App 3
Application Kind	Modern	Modern	Legacy
User Interface	Web Interface	API	Thick Client
Data Sensitivity	High	High	High
Compliance Requirements	HIPAA	None	None
Data Flow Diagrams (DFD)	Yes	No	No
Application Handles	Customer Data	PIIData	Intellectual Property
Business Impact	Critical	High	High
Threat Modelling	No	Yes	No
Security Testing	SAST & DAST	SCA, SAST & DAST	DAST
Business Owner	Andrew	John	Matt

Table 5

1) Asset Inventory Template: The Application Inventory template is a structured document used to catalogue key attributes of each application within an organization, including application type, user interface, data sensitivity, compliance requirements, and existing security controls. It serves as a foundational reference for security teams during threat modelling, test planning, and risk assessment by enabling informed decision-making and helping prioritize application security testing efforts based on business impact, regulatory exposure, and data flow characteristics. Maintaining this inventory ensures efficient risk assessment, better test planning, and comprehensive security coverage across the application landscape.
2) Applications that require security testing: Application security testing is essential for applications that handle sensitive data (e.g., personal, financial, or health information), are publicly accessible, or process critical

transactions. It ensures regulatory compliance (e.g., PCI DSS, HIPAA, GDPR) and protects against threats introduced through new features, tech stack changes, or third-party integrations. Security testing is also vital during audits, mergers, or modernization efforts to assess inherited risks and maintain robust access control.

3) Application-wise security testing objective and their compliance and regulatory requirements: Security testing objectives vary depending on the type, function and business of an application. Web applications require testing for input validation, authentication flaws, and session management to prevent OWASP Top 10 vulnerabilities, while mobile apps demand scrutiny of local data storage, API calls, and reverse engineering resistance. Cloud-native applications emphasize secure configurations, access control, and container isolation. Each application's compliance scope is shaped by its data handling responsibilities — applications processing personal data must align with GDPR and CCPA (California Consumer Privacy Act) while those handling health information are subject to HIPAA. Financial applications must meet PCI DSS standards, and apps influencing financial reporting fall under SOX.

4) Security testing team: A well-rounded security testing team consists of key specialized roles to ensure comprehensive coverage. The Security Test Manager drives the overall strategy, resource planning, and coordination across departments, aligning testing efforts with compliance goals. The Application Security Test Engineer (AppSec) focuses on code-level vulnerability detection through tools like SCA, SAST, DAST, and IAST, working closely with developers. A Penetration Tester mimics real-world attacks to expose weaknesses, while the Security Architect performs threat modelling and architecture reviews to design secure systems. Supporting these efforts, the

DevSecOps Engineer automates security into CI/CD pipelines, and the Compliance & Risk Officer ensures all testing aligns with regulatory frameworks like GDPR and PCI DSS.

Understanding Core Security Testing Methodologies:

Security testing is not a monolithic activity; it comprises several distinct approaches, each designed to find different types of vulnerabilities at various stages of the software development lifecycle (SDLC).

Secret Scanning

Concept

Secret scanning is the process of detecting sensitive data such as API keys, passwords, tokens, private keys, and other credentials within source code, configuration files, or repositories. It helps prevent accidental exposure of secrets that could lead to unauthorized access. Secret scanning tools identify hardcoded secrets and misconfigurations. This is crucial for maintaining application and infrastructure security.

When to use

Secret scanning should be integrated early in the Software Development Life Cycle (SDLC), particularly during the coding and commit stages. It is best used within CI/CD pipelines and source code repositories (e.g., GitHub, GitLab) to automatically detect secrets before they are pushed. It can also be part of pre-commit hooks or manual review processes.

Strengths

- Quickly detects accidentally committed secrets before they become a threat.
- Can be integrated and automated into IDEs and DevSecOps pipelines for continuous protection.
- Helps enforce secure coding practices and compliance with security standards.

- Reduces the attack surface by identifying secrets early in development.

Limitation

- May produce false positives, flagging non-secret strings as secrets.
- Limited to what patterns/signatures the scanner is configured to recognize — custom secrets may go undetected.
- Cannot detect secrets stored in encrypted or obfuscated formats.

Example

A developer accidentally commits an AWS access key into a public GitHub repository. A secret scanning tool detects the pattern of the key and alerts the team before attackers can exploit it.

1. **Static Application Security Testing (SAST):**
    - Concept: SAST analyses application source code, bytecode, or binary code for security vulnerabilities without actually executing the application. It automatically pinpoints and flags security vulnerabilities.
    - When to Use: Primarily used during the development and testing phases, it can also be used as a stand-alone also; however, for best outcomes, it should typically be integrated into the developer's Integrated Development Environment (IDE) or within CI/CD pipelines.
    - Strengths: Can find vulnerabilities early ("shift left"), pinpoint the exact line of code, and cover 100% of the code. Excellent for identifying common security vulnerabilities like SQL injection, cross-site scripting (XSS), insecure direct object references, and buffer overflows.

- Limitations: Can produce a high number of false positives; may not detect runtime configuration issues or flaws in third-party components unless specifically configured.

Example:

1) A SAST tool might flag the following Java code that uses string concatenation with unsanitized user input to construct an SQL query. This allows attackers to inject arbitrary SQL into the query:

String query = String.format("SELECT * FROM users WHERE id = %s", request.getParameter("id"));

2) A SAST tool might also flag the following case, where basic sanitization is attempted by escaping single quotes. However, this is still vulnerable because attackers can use alternate injection techniques (numeric-based payloads, comments, encodings, Boolean and UNION-based payloads, etc.) to bypass this defence:

String id = request.getParameter("id").replaceAll("'", "''");

String query = "SELECT * FROM users WHERE id = '" + id + "'";

In both cases, the SAST tool would raise a **SQL Injection** finding, highlighting the vulnerable lines in the Java code.

2. Dynamic Application Security Testing (DAST):

- Concept: DAST analyses the application in its running state, typically by simulating attacks from the outside, much like a real attacker would. It interacts with the application through its front-end interfaces (HTTP/S requests).
- When to Use: Used primarily in the testing or quality assurance (QA) environment, or even in production (with caution and proper scope).

- Strengths: Identifies vulnerabilities that are only apparent at runtime, such as configuration errors, server-side issues, authentication flaws, and certain business logic flaws. It is language-agnostic.
- Limitations: Cannot pinpoint the exact line of code (only the request/response), requires a running application, and might miss vulnerabilities in unexercised code paths.
    - Struggles with modern SPAs (single page applications)
    - Limited coverage of authenticated flows
    - Can't detect race conditions

Example: A DAST tool might discover an insecure session management flaw by attempting to replay a valid session token from a different user, or find an unpatched web server vulnerability that allows directory traversal.

3. **Software Composition Analysis (SCA):**
    - Concept: SCA tools identify and analyse open-source and third-party components used within an application. They check these components against known vulnerability databases (e.g., National Vulnerability Database - NVD) and license compliance issues.
    - When to Use: Early in the development process, during continuous integration, and regularly throughout the lifecycle to monitor for new vulnerabilities in existing dependencies.
    - Strengths: Crucial for managing supply chain risks, identifying publicly disclosed vulnerabilities (CVEs) in libraries, and ensuring license compliance. Use SCA to generate SBOMs and track dependency risk over time.

- Limitations: Only identifies known vulnerabilities; cannot find zero-day vulnerabilities in third-party components unless they are already disclosed.

Example: An SCA tool might flag an older version of a popular JavaScript library used in the frontend, indicating it contains a known critical XSS vulnerability that needs to be updated.

4. **Manual Security Review / Code Review:**
   - Concept: Humans with expertise in application security or trained developers manually examine code for security flaws, adherence to secure coding standards, and architectural weaknesses.
   - When to Use: Throughout the development process, particularly for critical components, complex logic, or sensitive areas of the application. Often complements automated SAST findings.
   - Strengths: Can identify complex logic flaws, business logic vulnerabilities, and subtle design issues that automated tools might miss. Provides deeper context and understanding.
   - Limitations: Scalability challenges, requires highly skilled personnel, can be costly and time-consuming.

Example: A manual review might uncover a flaw where a user can bypass a pricing logic by manipulating the order of operations in the application's API calls, a type of issue often missed by automated scanners.

5. **Penetration Testing (Pen testing):**
   - Concept: A simulated cyberattack against an application, system, or network to check for exploitable vulnerabilities. Performed by independent security experts (ethical hackers).

- When to Use: Typically performed once the application is largely complete or before major releases, and often annually for critical applications, to validate the overall security posture and meet compliance requirements.
- Strengths: Provides a real-world perspective on exploitable vulnerabilities, combines findings from various testing types, and often uncovers chained attacks.
- Limitations: Point-in-time assessment (snapshot), can be expensive and resource-intensive, and does not provide continuous coverage.

Example: A pen tester might exploit an authentication bypass vulnerability to gain unauthorized access, then leverage a local file inclusion flaw to execute malicious code on the server, demonstrating a critical attack chain.

Initial Focus: For establishing basics, organizations should prioritize integrating Secret Scanning, Software Composition Analysis (SCA) and SAST Scans into their developer workflows and CI/CD pipelines as early as possible. DAST can follow for more comprehensive runtime analysis. Manual reviews and penetration testing should be scheduled for critical applications as resources allow.

4.2 Tool Selection and Implementation

The market for application security testing (AST) tools is vast and rapidly evolving. Selecting the right tools and implementing them effectively is crucial for building a scalable and efficient AppSec program. This isn't about acquiring the most expensive tools, but rather choosing those that best fit the organization's needs, development stack, maturity level, and budget.

Key Considerations for Tool Selection:

1. Development Stack Compatibility: The chosen tools must seamlessly integrate with the programming languages, frameworks, build systems, and IDEs used by development teams.

2. Accuracy and False Positive Rate: While no tool is perfect, a high rate of false positives (reporting vulnerabilities that aren't real) leads to "overly frequent warnings" and erodes developer trust. Conversely, a high false negative rate (missing real vulnerabilities) leaves critical gaps. Look for tools that offer good precision and recall.

3. Integration Capabilities: How well does the tool integrate with existing SDLC tools (e.g., Jira for defect tracking, Jenkins/GitLab CI for CI/CD, GitHub/GitLab for SCM)? Smooth integration is key to reducing friction.

4. Scalability and Performance: Can the tool handle the volume of code and applications the organization has now and in the future? Will scans run quickly enough to provide rapid feedback without delaying development cycles?

5. Reporting and Analytics: Does the tool provide clear, actionable reports? Can it track metrics over time, visualize trends, and support compliance reporting?

6. Usability and Developer Experience: Is the tool easy for developers to use and understand its findings? Tools that provide in-IDE feedback or clear remediation guidance are often preferred.

7. Cost and Licensing Model: Understand the total cost of ownership, including licensing, maintenance, training, and potential consulting fees.

8. Support and Community: What kind of vendor support is available? Is there an active community for shared knowledge and troubleshooting?

Common Tool Categories and Examples (Non-exhaustive):

Tool Category	Purpose	Example Commercial Tools	Example Open-Source/Free Tools
SAST	Analyses source code for vulnerabilities.	Fortify, Checkmarx, SonarQube (commercial features)	SonarQube (community edition), Bandit (Python), ESLint (JavaScript) GolangCI-Lint (for Go projects), MobSF (android/iOS source/binaries)
DAST	Tests running applications for vulnerabilities.	Acunetix, Invicti (Netsparker), Burp Suite Enterprise	OWASP ZAP, Nikto
SCA	Identifies and manages open-source component vulnerabilities.	Snyk, Black Duck, Mend (WhiteSource)	OWASP Dependency-Check, Retire.js
IAST	Analyses running applications from inside the app.	Contrast Security, HCL AppScan (some IAST features)	AIAST(Advanced interactive application security tool), Contrast ADR(community edition)
RASP	Runtime Application Self-Protection.	Imperva Runtime Protection, Contrast Security	ModSecurity (WAF-like)

Secret Detection	Finds hardcoded secrets (API keys, passwords).	GitGuardian, Semgrep	TruffleHog, Gitleaks

Table 6

Initial Implementation Strategy:

1. Start Small (Pilot Program): Do not try to implement tools across all applications simultaneously. Choose one or two non-critical but representative applications for a pilot. This allows for:
    - Learning how to configure and tune the tool effectively.
    - Understanding the typical false positive rate and how to manage it.
    - Gathering feedback from developers on usability and impact.
    - Demonstrating initial value before a wider rollout.
2. Define a Minimum Viable Security (MVS) Gate: For initial integration, set a clear but achievable security gate. For example, "No critical SAST findings can be introduced in new code," or "All new dependencies must pass SCA checks." This provides immediate feedback and prevents the accumulation of major debt.
3. Focus on Automation Early: Wherever possible, automate the tool execution. Manual processes are unsustainable and prone to human error. Integrate Secrets/SCA/SAST into the existing CI/CD pipelines to run automatically on every code commit or pull request.
4. Prioritize Remediation Guidance: Tools that simply report vulnerabilities are less effective than those that provide

clear, actionable remediation advice. Train developers on how to interpret findings and fix them. Consider integrating tools directly into developer IDEs for immediate feedback.

5. Iterate and Optimize: Tool selection and implementation are not one-time events. Regularly review tool effectiveness, explore new capabilities, and adjust configurations based on feedback and evolving needs.

By carefully selecting and strategically implementing foundational security testing tools, an organization can begin to proactively identify and address vulnerabilities, setting the stage for more advanced security practices.

4.3 Building a Security-Aware Culture

Even the most sophisticated tools and processes are insufficient without a strong foundation of human awareness and commitment. Building a security-aware culture means instilling a shared sense of responsibility for security across the entire organization, transforming it from a "security team's problem" into "everyone's job." This cultural shift is paramount for long-term success in application security.

Why Culture is Paramount:

- Human Element as Weakest Link: As highlighted in Chapter 2, human error and negligence are significant factors in data breaches. A security-aware culture reduces these risks by making security a conscious part of daily activities.
- Scalability: A small security team cannot review every line of code or every application. Empowering developers and other stakeholders to own security scales the program organically.
- Faster Remediation: Developers who understand security principles are more likely to write secure code from the outset and fix vulnerabilities faster when identified.

- Innovation with Security: When security is embedded in the culture, it becomes part of the innovation process, rather than a barrier to it. Developers are empowered to build secure products quickly.

- Sustained Security: Tools change, threats evolve, but a strong security culture fosters continuous learning and adaptation.

Strategies for Cultivating a Security-Aware Culture:

1. Leadership Buy-in and Sponsorship: Security culture starts at the top. Executives must actively champion security, communicate its importance, and visibly participate in security initiatives. Their commitment signals to the rest of the organization that security is a strategic priority.

Example: A CTO regularly mentioning application security in all-hands meetings, or a CISO presenting security metrics to the board, demonstrates strong leadership commitment.

2. Establish a Security Champions Program: This is one of the most effective ways to scale security knowledge and ownership.
    - Concept: Identify enthusiastic, respected developers or engineers within each development team who are interested in security. Train them thoroughly on secure coding, threat modelling, and security tools.

    - Role: These "champions" act as embedded security experts, providing first-line security advice to their teams, evangelizing secure practices, assisting with vulnerability triage, and acting as a liaison between development and the central security testing team.

    - Benefits: Reduces the bottleneck on the central security testing team, fosters a bottom-up approach, and integrates security into daily team dynamics.

3. Regular, Relevant, and Engaging Training:
    - Move beyond annual, generic cybersecurity awareness training.
    - Targeted Training: Provide role-specific training. For developers, focus on secure coding practices relevant to their tech stack (e.g., Python security, Java security, web security essentials like OWASP Top 10). For product managers, focus on security requirements and privacy by design.
    - Hands-on Labs and Gamification: Make training interactive and memorable. Secure Coding Challenges (CTFs - Capture The Flag), Hackathons, or Gamified Platforms (e.g., Secure Code Warrior, OWASP Juice Shop or Web Goat) can make learning fun and practical.
    - Just-in-Time Learning: Provide short, easily digestible modules that developers can access when they need them, perhaps linked directly from security tool findings.
4. Effective Internal Communications:
    - Regularly share updates, success stories, and lessons learned (without shaming) through internal newsletters, security blogs, or dedicated Slack channels.
    - Highlight Positive Behaviour: Recognize and reward teams or individuals who demonstrate exceptional security practices or contribute to security improvements.
    - Communicate the "Why": Always explain the business impact and personal relevance of security decisions, not just the technical requirements.

5. Foster Collaboration and Psychological Safety:
   - Create an environment where developers feel comfortable asking security questions, reporting potential vulnerabilities, and admitting mistakes without fear of blame.
   - Encourage cross-functional meetings between security, development, and operations.
   - "Blameless Post-Mortems": When security incidents occur, focus on process and system improvements, not individual blame.
6. Integrate Security into Performance Reviews (Carefully):
   - While not punitive, subtly incorporating secure coding practices or participation in security initiatives into performance goals can reinforce their importance. This should be done with a focus on growth and positive reinforcement.

Example Cultural Initiative:
A large tech firm is implementing a "Security Guild" program to foster a bottom-up approach to security awareness. This initiative involves:

- **Cross-functional Guilds:** Small, voluntary groups of employees from various departments (development, operations, HR, marketing, even sales) who will meet regularly to discuss security topics relevant to their roles.
- **"Security Story Time" Sessions:** Monthly informal gatherings where employees shared real-world examples of security challenges they faced, how they resolved them, or lessons learned from minor incidents (without blame). This would create a safe space for learning.
- **"Bug Bounty Light" Internal Program:** Employees are encouraged to report any perceived security weaknesses,

even if minor (e.g., a suspicious email, a potential misconfiguration, an odd login prompt), to a dedicated internal team. They will receive small, non-monetary rewards (e.g., gift cards, extra PTO) for valid findings, shifting the mindset from "reporting problems" to "contributing to solutions."

- **Security Champion Network:** The Guilds naturally identified passionate individuals who could become departmental security champions, acting as local points of contact and advocates for security best practices within their teams.

This program shifted security from being solely an "IT problem" to a shared responsibility, empowering employees to proactively identify and address risks in their daily work. It built a strong sense of collective ownership and made security a topic of regular, open discussion rather than just a compliance mandate.

4.4 Initial Risk Assessment & Baseline Metrics

Before an organization can effectively improve its application security, it must first understand its current state of risk and establish measurable baselines. This involves identifying the most critical applications, assessing their existing vulnerabilities, and defining the key performance indicators (KPIs) that will track progress. This initial assessment provides the necessary data to prioritize efforts, justify investments, and demonstrate the value of the security program over time.

Purpose of Initial Risk Assessment:

1. Identify Critical Assets: Not all applications are equally important. Identify the applications that handle sensitive data (e.g., customer PII, financial data, intellectual property), support critical business functions, or are publicly exposed. Use an application/asset inventory

template. These applications will be the initial focus for security efforts.

2. Understand Current Risk Posture: Get a snapshot of existing vulnerabilities across the identified critical applications. This includes both known (e.g., OWASP Top 10) and unknown (e.g., business logic flaws) vulnerabilities.
3. Justify Investment: Quantify the current risks to demonstrate the urgent need for security improvements and secure resources for the program.
4. Establish a Starting Point: Create a measurable baseline against which future improvements can be compared.

Methodologies for Initial Risk Assessment:

1. **Application Inventory and Classification:**
   - Create a comprehensive inventory of all applications, internal and external.
   - Classify the applications based on criticality (e.g., business impact, data sensitivity, regulatory requirements).

Example Classification Table:

Classification	Business Impact	Data Sensitivity	Regulatory Implication	Examples
Critical	High	Highly Sensitive (PHI, PCI, PII)	Strict (GDPR, HIPAA, PCI DSS)	Online banking, healthcare portal, payment gateway
High	Medium-High	Sensitive (Internal PII, proprietary data)	Moderate	CRM, internal HR system, core internal business apps

Medium	Medium	Confidential (General business data)	General	Project management tools, internal wiki, corporate website
Low	Low	Public/non-sensitive	Minimal	Public marketing site (static), internal non-sensitive tools

Table 7

Targeted Vulnerability Scanning and Penetration Testing:

- Begin with automated scans (Secrets scanning, SCA, SAST, DAST,) on the *most critical* applications identified in the inventory. This provides a quick way to uncover prevalent vulnerabilities.
- Consider a focused, initial penetration test for the top 1-2 most critical applications to gain a realistic understanding of exploitable risks.

Example: Run a SAST scan on the core and critical application's codebase and a DAST scan on its staging environment. This immediately reveals known coding flaws and runtime configuration issues.

2. **Simplified Threat Modelling:**
    - Conduct basic threat modelling workshops for a few critical applications. Focus on identifying key assets, potential attackers, and common attack vectors. This helps teams start thinking adversely.

Example: For a new customer onboarding application, a simple threat model might identify that the user registration API is a critical asset, and "unauthenticated attackers" might try "account enumeration" or "injection attacks."

3. **Review Existing Security Controls and Documentation:**
   - Assess existing security policies, architectural diagrams, security controls (e.g., WAFs, IDS/IPS), and past audit reports. Identify gaps and areas of non-compliance.

Defining Baseline Metrics:

Once the initial assessments are complete, establish baseline metrics that will allow for quantitative tracking of improvement over time. These should be linked to the long-term objectives.

Mean Time to Detect (MTTD)

MTTD is the average time it takes for an organization to identify a security vulnerability or incident from the moment it occurs or is introduced into the system.

While detection and remediation rates focus on the quantity of vulnerabilities, Mean Time to Detect (MTTD) introduces the crucial element of speed. It reflects how quickly an organization can identify a security event or vulnerability and subsequently neutralize the threat.

- Vulnerability Metrics:
  - Average number of critical/high severity vulnerabilities per application (per type: Secret Scanning, SCA, SAST, DAST). This is a direct measure of the initial security debt.
  - Vulnerability density: Number of critical/high-severity vulnerabilities per 1,000 lines of code (LoC) or per application.
  - Percentage of applications with at least one critical/high vulnerability.

- Time-to-Remediate (TTR) Metrics:
  - Mean Time to Remediate (MTTR) critical/high vulnerabilities. The average time it takes from discovery to fix in production. This shows remediation efficiency.

- Coverage Metrics:
  - Percentage of critical applications scanned by Secrets/SCA/SAST/DAST.
  - Percentage of code repositories with integrated security scanning.

- Cultural/Process Metrics (Initial):
  - Percentage of developers who have completed baseline security awareness training.
  - Number of reported security defects (even if low initially, indicates awareness).

Example Baseline Snapshot:

Metric	**Baseline (Q1 2025)**	**Target (Q1 2026)**
Avg. Critical/High severity Vulns (per one critical app)	15 (SAST), 5 (DAST), 8 (SCA)	10 (SAST), 3 (DAST), 2 (SCA)
MTTR Critical Vulns (overall)	60 days	30 days
% Critical Apps with SAST/SCA in CI/CD	20%	60%
% Developers with Basic Security Training	30%	80%

Table 8

These baseline metrics provide a concrete starting point. They help in articulating the problem to stakeholders, prioritizing initial efforts (e.g., focusing on critical applications with high vulnerability counts), and measuring the success of Phase 1 initiatives before moving to deeper integration.

Phase 2: Integration

Once the foundational elements are in place, Phase 2 focuses on deeply embedding security into the daily fabric of the software development lifecycle. This is where the "shift-left" philosophy truly takes hold, moving security from a separate gate to an inherent part of how software is designed, built, and delivered.

4.5 Embedding Security into SDLC

Embedding security into the SDLC, often termed DevSecOps, means integrating security testing activities, tools, and responsibilities throughout every stage of software development, rather than just treating it as a final checklist item. This proactive approach aims to identify and remediate vulnerabilities early, when they are significantly cheaper and easier to fix.

The "Shift Left" Paradigm:
The core principle is to "shift left" — move security considerations and testing activities as early as possible in the SDLC. The cost of fixing a bug increases exponentially the later it is discovered (Source: IBM Systems Sciences Institute):

- Requirements/Design Phase: Cost = $1
- Development/Coding Phase: Cost = $10
- Testing Phase: Cost = $100
- Production/Post-Release: Cost = $1,000+ (plus potential breach costs)

By shifting left, organizations can catch flaws at the architectural or coding stage, where the cost of remediation is minimal.

Integrating Security into Each SDLC Phase:

1. Planning and Requirements:

- Activity: Define clear security requirements for each application and feature. Incorporate security from the outset, alongside functional requirements.
- Tools/Techniques: Use frameworks like OWASP Application Security Verification Standard (ASVS) or custom security design requirement checklists. Conduct initial privacy impact assessments (PIAs) and data protection impact assessments (DPIAs).

Example: For a new user authentication module, a security requirement might be: "The system MUST support multi-factor authentication (MFA) for all user roles, and password hashing MUST use a strong, industry-standard algorithm like bcrypt with a minimum work factor of 12."

2. Design and Architecture:
   - Activity: Conduct threat modelling workshops. Identify potential attack surfaces, threats, and vulnerabilities in the design before any code is written. Design secure architectures, consider secure defaults, and employ secure design patterns.
   - Tools/Techniques: STRIDE/ DREAD methodology, Data Flow Diagrams (DFDs), architectural security reviews.

Example: During the design of an application architecture, threat modelling identifies that API could be vulnerable to Fuzzing, Parameter Tampering, and Rate Limiting. The design is then updated to enforce mutual proper input validations on all API's.

3. Development and Coding:
   - Activity: Empower developers with secure coding knowledge and integrate security testing tools directly into their daily workflow.
   - Tools/Techniques: Secure coding guidelines, in-IDE SAST plugins, pre-commit hooks for secret detection, mandatory peer code reviews with security-focused checklists.

Example: A developer writing new code receives an immediate alert in their IDE from a SAST plugin, flagging an unsafe deserialization vulnerability as they type, prompting them to fix it before committing.

4. Testing and Quality Assurance:
   - Activity: Incorporate automated security testing into continuous integration (CI) pipelines and dedicated security testing in staging environments.
   - Tools/Techniques: Automated Secret Scanning, SCA, SAST, and DAST scans run with every build or pull request. Dedicated penetration testing for major releases.

Example: A pull request triggers automated Secret Scans, SCA Scans and SAST Scans. If critical vulnerabilities are found, the build is automatically "stopped," preventing the insecure code from being merged into the main branch.

5. Deployment:
   - Activity: Ensure secure deployment configurations, manage secrets securely, and apply infrastructure-as-code security validations.
   - Tools/Techniques: Configuration management tools (Ansible, Chef), secret management solutions (HashiCorp Vault, AWS Secrets Manager), IaC security scanners (Checkov, Terrascan).

Example: A deployment pipeline includes a step to scan the Kubernetes YAML configuration files for security misconfigurations before deploying the application to production.

6. Operations and Monitoring:
   - Activity: Continuously monitor applications in production for security incidents, new vulnerabilities, and anomalous behaviour. Establish robust incident response plans.

- Tools/Techniques: Runtime Application Self-Protection (RASP), Web Application Firewalls (WAFs), Security Information and Security Incident and Event Management (SIEM) systems, logging, and alerting.

Example: A RASP solution deployed with a critical production application detects and blocks an attempted SQL injection attack in real-time, preventing a breach and alerting the security operations centre.

By systematically integrating security into each phase, organizations can build security in from the start, reduce their attack surface, and make application security an intrinsic part of delivering value.

4.6 Developer Training & Secure Coding Practices

Developers are on the front lines of software creation, and their understanding of security principles is paramount to building secure applications. Effective developer training and the institutionalization of secure coding practices are cornerstones of a successful application security program. This goes beyond generic cybersecurity awareness and delves into practical, actionable guidance tailored to their daily work.

Why Focus on Developers?

- Root Cause Remediation: Developers are best positioned to fix security flaws at their source – in the code.
- Preventive Measures: Training empowers developers to write secure code from the start, reducing the number of vulnerabilities introduced.
- Scalability: A large developer workforce, when security-aware, becomes a distributed security team, multiplying the organization's defensive capabilities.
- Reduced Cost: Fixing bugs during coding is dramatically cheaper than fixing them later in the SDLC or after a breach.

Types of Developer Training:

1. Foundational Secure Coding Principles:
   - Content: Cover core security concepts, common vulnerability types (e.g., OWASP Top 10), and general secure coding best practices that apply across languages.
   - Format: Online modules, interactive workshops, presentations.
   - Frequency: Mandatory for all new developers; annual refreshers for existing teams.

2. Language/Framework-Specific Secure Coding:
   - Content: Deep dive into security considerations for specific programming languages (e.g., Java, Python, Node.js), frameworks (e.g., Spring Boot, React, Django), and database technologies. Address common pitfalls and secure alternatives within those ecosystems.
   - Format: Hands-on labs, code examples, pair programming exercises.

Example: Training for Java developers would cover prevention of Log4Shell-like vulnerabilities, secure deserialization in Java, and secure use of JDBC. For React developers, it might focus on preventing XSS via proper rendering, secure API calls, and protecting against client-side tampering.

3. Threat Modelling Workshops:
   - Content: Train developers and architects on how to conduct basic threat modelling for their applications. Focus on identifying assets, threats, vulnerabilities, and countermeasures.
   - Format: Collaborative workshops, often led by a security architect.
   - Benefit: Enables developers to think adversarially and design security in from the design phase.

4. Security Tool Training:
   - Content: How to use the organization's specific SAST, SCA, and DAST tools effectively. How to interpret their findings, differentiate between true positives and false positives, and access remediation guidance.
   - Format: Tool-specific demos, hands-on practice, documentation.

5. Gamified Learning & Challenges:
   - Content: Interactive platforms that present real-world insecure code challenges, allowing developers to find and fix vulnerabilities in a safe environment.
   - Format: Capture The Flag (CTF) events, secure coding competitions, platforms like Secure Code Warrior or OWASP Juice Shop.
   - Benefit: Makes learning engaging, practical, and fosters a competitive spirit around security.

Establishing Secure Coding Practices:

Beyond formal training, organizations need to embed secure coding practices into their daily development workflows.

1. Secure Coding Guidelines:
   - Develop and publish clear, concise, and accessible secure coding guidelines specific to the organization's tech stack. Refer to industry standards like OWASP Cheat Sheet Series.

Example: A guideline might state: "All user input must be validated and sanitized on the server-side before being used in database queries or displayed in the UI."

2. Automated Secure Code Analysis (SAST, SCA):
   - Integrate SAST and SCA tools into developer IDEs and CI/CD pipelines. This provides immediate, "just-in-time" feedback on security flaws.

Example: A developer types a piece of code, and their IDE's SAST plugin immediately flags a potential vulnerability, suggesting a secure alternative, allowing them to fix it before even committing the code.

3. Security-Focused Code Reviews:
    - Incorporate security as a mandatory aspect of peer code reviews. Developers reviewing code should actively look for security flaws, not just functional bugs.

Checklist: Provide a simple security checklist for reviewers to follow during code reviews.

4. Secure by Design Libraries/Frameworks:
    - Promote the use of internal or external libraries and frameworks that are designed with security in mind (e.g., ORMs that prevent SQL injection, secure authentication libraries).
    - Discourage the use of known insecure functions or patterns.

5. Security Champions Network:
    - As mentioned in 4.3, security champions act as local experts, providing informal training, answering questions, and promoting secure practices within their teams.

By investing in comprehensive developer training and consistently reinforcing secure coding practices through tooling and processes, organizations can significantly reduce the introduction of new vulnerabilities and foster a strong, proactive security posture from the ground up.

4.7 Continuous Testing in CI/CD Pipelines

To truly "shift left" and achieve agility with security, continuous security testing must be deeply integrated into the Continuous Integration/Continuous Delivery (CI/CD) pipelines. This automation ensures that security checks are not a bottleneck but an inherent, rapid feedback mechanism for developers, allowing vulnerabilities to be identified and remediated almost as soon as they are introduced.

The Role of CI/CD in AppSec:

CI/CD pipelines automate the build, test, and deployment processes. Integrating security tools into these pipelines means:

- Automated Execution: Security scans run automatically without manual intervention.
- Rapid Feedback: Developers receive immediate feedback on security flaws, often within minutes of committing code.
- Consistent Application: Every code change undergoes the same security scrutiny.
- Prevention of Build Breakage: Critical vulnerabilities can be set to "break/stop the build," preventing insecure code from progressing to later stages.

Integration Points and Tools in the CI/CD Pipeline:

SDLC Stage	Integration Point	Security Tooling	Purpose/Benefit
Code Commit / Pre-Commit	Developer Workstation / Git Hook	Linting tools, Secret Scanners (e.g., Gitleaks), in-IDE SAST	Catch simple syntax errors, hardcoded secrets, and basic vulnerabilities before code is even committed. Fastest feedback loop.

Code Build / Pull Request	CI Server (e.g., Jenkins, GitLab CI, GitHub Actions)	SAST, SCA, Code Linting, Unit Tests (with security assertions)	Automated analysis of source code and dependencies. Critical vulnerabilities can fail the build, preventing the merge.
Component / Image Creation	Image Registry / CI Build	Container Security Scanning (e.g., Snyk)	Scan Docker images for known vulnerabilities in OS, packages, and application layers before deployment.
Deployment to Staging/Test	CD Pipeline / Test Environment	DAST, IAST, Security Unit/Integration Tests	Test the running application for vulnerabilities, configuration issues, and runtime flaws. More realistic attack simulation.
Post-Deployment / Runtime	Production Environment	RASP, WAF, SIEM, Continuous DAST (optional)	Real-time protection against attacks, monitoring for suspicious activity, and continuous validation of security posture.

Table 9

Key Strategies for Continuous Testing:

1. "Break/Stop the Build" for Critical Issues: Configure the CI/CD pipeline to fail the build if critical or high-severity vulnerabilities are detected by SAST or SCA tools. This enforces security gates early.

Example: A developer pushes code, the SAST scan runs, and finds a critical SQL injection vulnerability. The build fails immediately, and the developer receives an alert with details, forcing them to fix it before merging their changes.

2. Optimize Scan Times: Integrate lightweight, fast scans at the earliest stages (e.g., quick SAST scans on feature branches) and longer, more comprehensive scans on main branches or nightly builds. This balances speed with thoroughness.

3. Manage False Positives: Work with development teams to triage and manage false positives from automated tools. Over time, tune the tools, use rulesets integrated with organizational secure code framework and create baselines to reduce noise, ensuring developers trust the findings.

4. Centralized Reporting: Consolidate results from various security tools into a single dashboard or defect tracking system (e.g., Jira). This provides a unified view of the application's security posture and helps prioritize remediation.

5. Security Unit and Integration Tests: Encourage developers to write security-focused tests (e.g., test cases that try to bypass authentication, or validate input sanitization) as part of their regular unit and integration testing. These tests can run with every commit.

6. Automated Security Gates: Implement automated gates based on predefined policies. For example, "no new critical

SAST findings," "SCA allows only dependencies with 'medium' or lower severity known vulnerabilities," or "DAST scan must complete with zero critical findings."

Example CI/CD Workflow with Integrated Security:

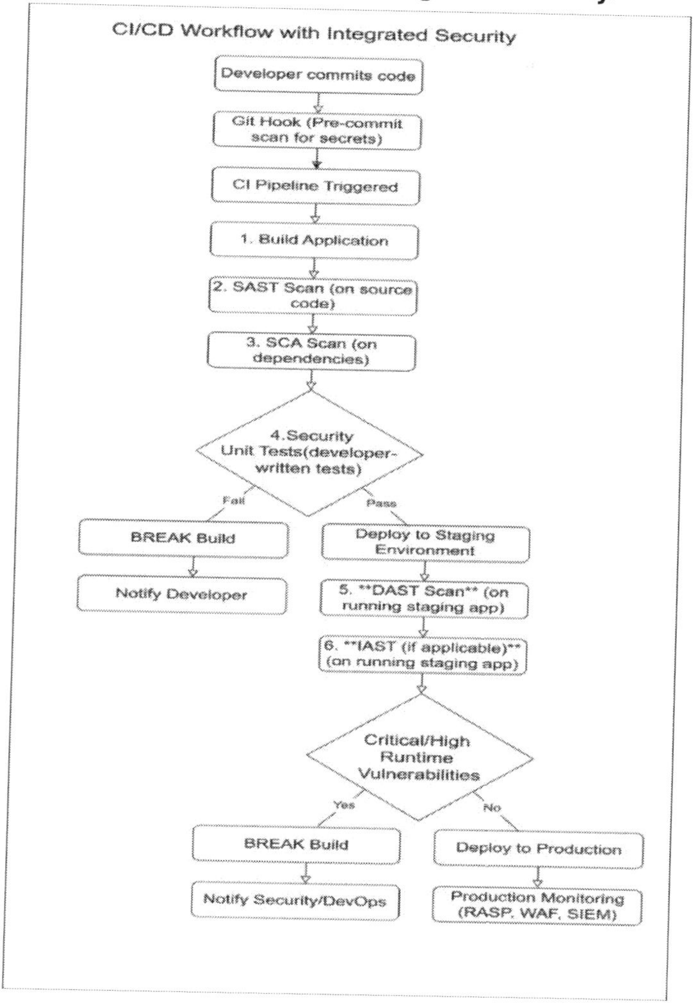

Figure 1

This integrated approach ensures that security is an active, continuous part of the development and delivery process, fostering a "security-first" mindset and reducing the likelihood of vulnerabilities making their way into production.

4.8 Threat Modelling & Risk Prioritization

While automated tools are excellent at finding known vulnerability patterns, they often miss business logic flaws, design weaknesses, and subtle interactions that create unique attack vectors. This is where threat modelling becomes indispensable. Coupled with risk prioritization, it ensures that an organization focuses its limited security resources on the most impactful threats to its most critical assets.

What is Threat Modelling?

Threat modelling is a structured process used to identify potential threats, vulnerabilities, and countermeasure requirements for a system or application. It is a proactive approach, ideally performed early in the SDLC (design phase), but can also be applied to existing applications. The goal is to understand *how* an attacker might compromise the system and *what* the impact would be.

Steps for Threat Modelling:

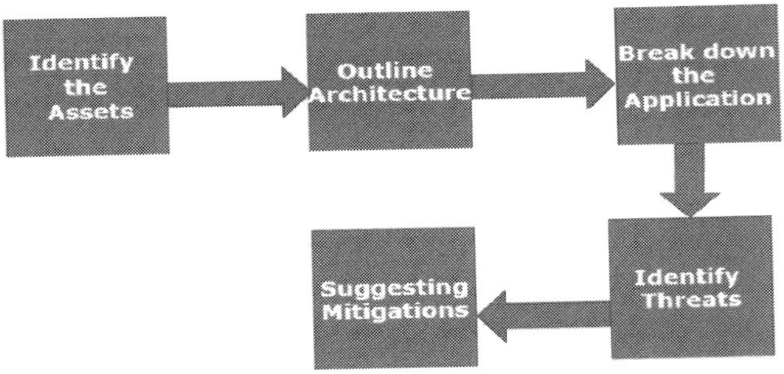

Figure 2

Common Threat Modelling Methodologies:

1. **STRIDE**: (Microsoft's model)
   - Focus: Categorizes threats based on different security properties:
     - Spoofing (authentication)
     - Tampering (integrity)
     - Repudiation (non-repudiation)
     - Information Disclosure (confidentiality)
     - Denial of Service (availability)
     - Elevation of Privilege (authorization)

STRIDE Table:

Type	Description	Security Control
Spoofing	Threat action aimed at accessing and use of another user's credentials, such as username and password.	Authentication
Tampering	Threat action intending to maliciously change or modify persistent data, such as records in a database, and the alteration of data in transit between two computers over an open network, such as the Internet.	Integrity
Repudiation	Threat action aimed at performing prohibited	Non-Repudiation

	operations in a system that lacks the ability to trace the operations.	
Information disclosure	Threat action intending to read a file that one was not granted access to, or to read data in transit.	Confidentiality
Denial of service	Threat action attempting to deny access to valid users, such as by making a web server temporarily unavailable or unusable.	Availability
Elevation of privilege	Threat action intending to gain privileged access to resources in order to gain unauthorized access to information or to compromise a system.	Authorization

Table 10

- Process: Often applied to Data Flow Diagrams (DFDs) to identify threats at various trust boundaries.
- Benefit: Provides a systematic way to enumerate common threat types.

Example

Let's take a sample web application with a login functionality and a database. Here is the Data Flow Diagram (DFD) for the sample application

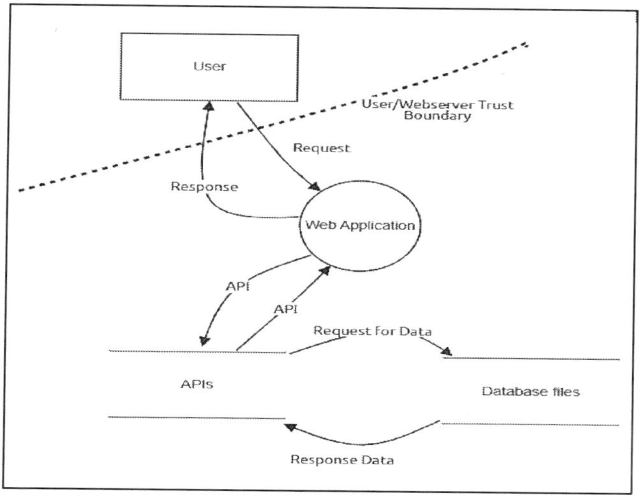

Figure 3

Use and Misuse Case Graphs:

a) Use and Misuse Case Graph for Authentication (Spoofing):

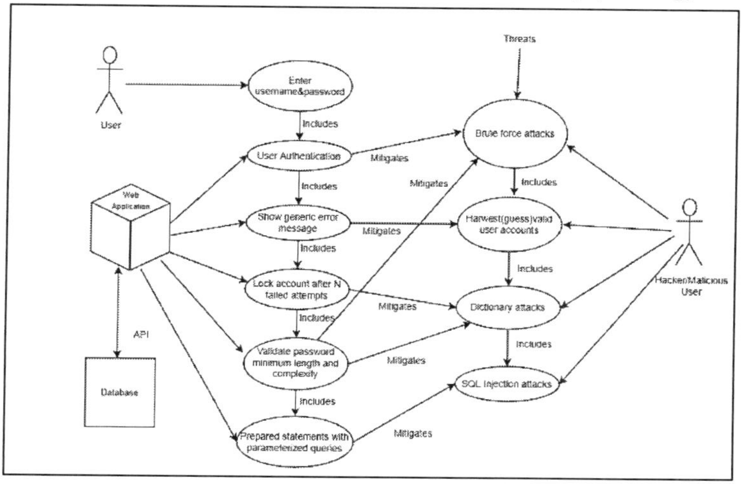

Figure 4

b) Use and Misuse Case Graph for Integrity (Tampering):

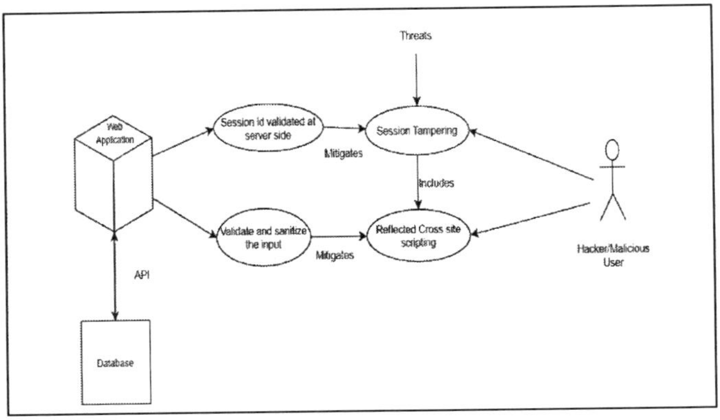

Figure 5

c) Use and Misuse Case Graph for Non-Repudiation (Repudiation):

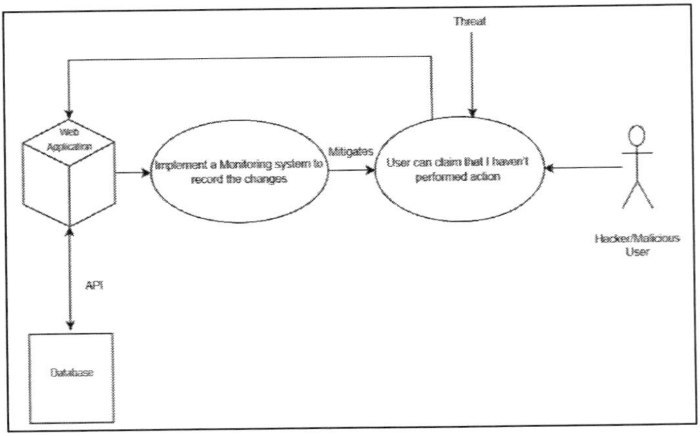

Figure 6

d) Use and Misuse Case Graph for Confidentiality (Information Disclosure):

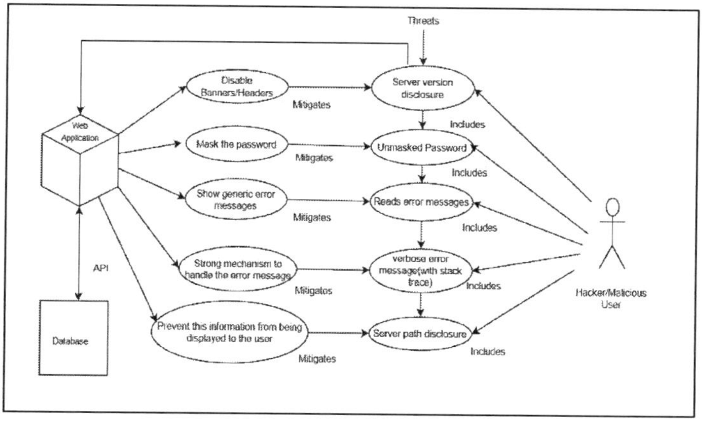

Figure 7

e) Use and Misuse Case Graph for Availability (Denial of Service):

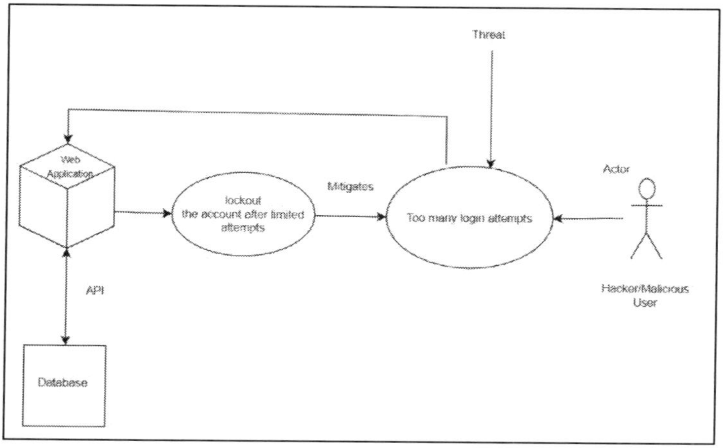

Figure 8

f) Use and Misuse Case Graph for Authorization (Elevation of Privilege):

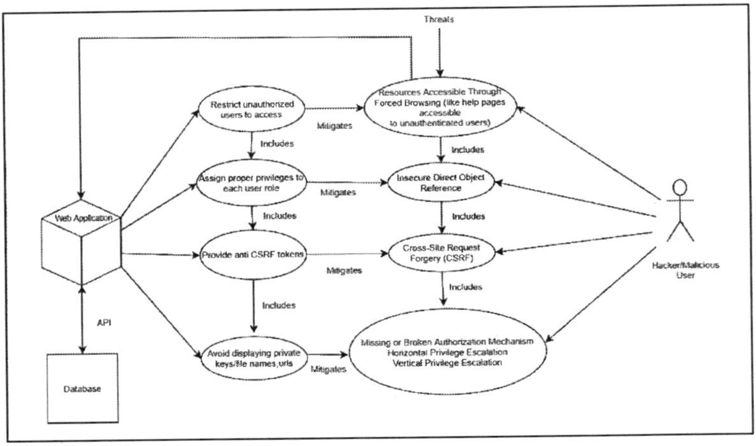

Figure 9

g) Use and Misuse Case Graph for API Issues:

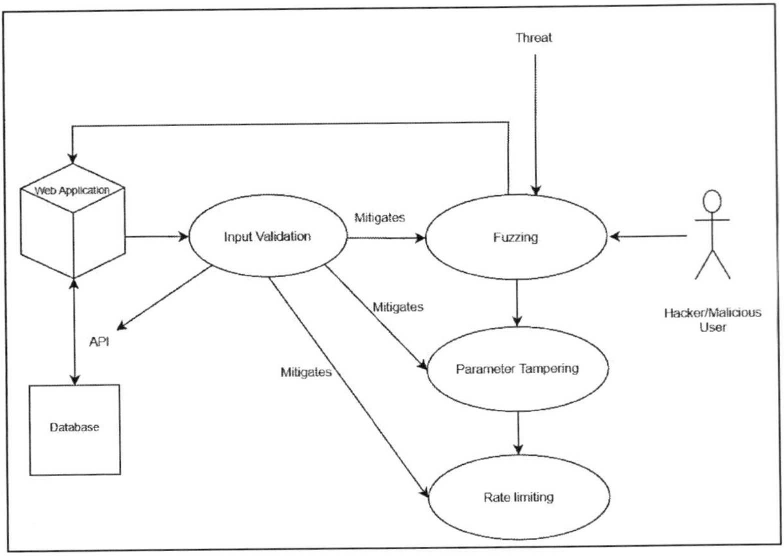

Figure 10

1. Threats Identified:

S. No	Application Component	Threats*	Mitigation
1	Login	Dictionary Attacks	Lock account after "N*" failed attempts
2	Application	Sensitive Information Disclosure	Show generic error messages
3	Application	Repudiation	Implement monitoring
4	Application	Cross Site Request Forgery	Use Anti CSRF tokens
5	Application	SQL Injection	Use parameterized queries
6	Application	Cross Site Scripting (XSS)	Output encoding and input sanitization
7	Application	Insecure Direct Object Reference	Validate user permissions for resource access
8	Application	Unvalidated Redirects and Forwards	Validate and whitelist redirect URLs
9	Application	Broken Access Control	Enforce role-based access checks
10	Application	XML External entry [XXE]	Disable external entities in XML parsers
11	Application	Use of Vulnerable Components	Regularly update dependencies and libraries
12	Login page and Forgot Password	Denial of service	Lock out the account
13	API	Fuzzing	Input Validation
14	API	Parameter Tampering	Input Validation
15	API	Lack of Rate Limiting	Apply rate limiting

Table 11

N*=number of failed login attempts.

Threats*= Indicate sample threats only and do not represent a comprehensive list of all possible threats.

2. DREAD: ()

DREAD Threat List:

Type	Description	Security Control
Damage Potential	Measures how much damage the exploit could cause to the system or business.	Data loss prevention, impact mitigation plans
Reproducibility	Measures how easy it is to reproduce the attack.	Code obfuscation, rate limiting
Exploitability	Measures how easy it is to launch the attack.	Patch management, secure configuration
Affected Users	Measures how many users would be affected if the threat is exploited.	Segmentation, user scope limitations
Discoverability	Measures how easy it is to discover the threat or vulnerability.	Security by design, hidden endpoints

Table 12

- Focus: A qualitative risk assessment model for discovered threats:
  - Damage potential
  - Reproducibility
  - Exploitability
  - Affected users
  - Discoverability
- Benefit: Helps in prioritizing identified threats for remediation.

3. PASTA: (Process for Attack Simulation and Threat Analysis)

Stage	Description	Security Control
Stage 1: Define Objectives	Identify business and security goals.	Security requirement gathering, policy definitions
Stage 2: Define Technical Scope	Analyses system architecture, applications, interfaces, and dependencies.	Asset inventory, architecture documentation
Stage 3: Application Decomposition	Decompose the app into data flows, components, and trust boundaries.	Data Flow Diagrams (DFDs), trust boundary identification
Stage 4: Threat Analysis	Identify and map potential threats to the system (based on STRIDE, CAPEC, etc.).	Threat intelligence integration, STRIDE, CAPEC mapping
Stage 5: Vulnerability & Weakness Analysis	Map application and infrastructure vulnerabilities to threats using methods like threat trees, then categorize and score them using CVE/CWE and CVSS/CWSS.	Vulnerability scanning (SAST/DAST), pentesting
Stage 6: Attack Modelling & Simulation	Simulate real-world attack scenarios using threat actor profiles and TTPs.	Threat emulation, MITRE ATT&CK framework
Stage 7: Risk & Impact Analysis	Assess risk levels and business impact from successful threat exploitation.	Risk scoring models, business continuity planning

Table 13

- Focus: A seven-stage, risk-centric methodology that integrates business context with technical analysis.
- Stages: Defines objectives, defines technical scope, decomposes application, analyses threats, analyses vulnerabilities, analyses attacks, and analyses risk and impact.
- Benefit: Provides a comprehensive, business-driven approach to threat modelling.

Attack Trees:

- Focus: A hierarchical diagram that breaks down a high-level attack goal into more specific sub-goals and underlying methods.
- Benefit: Visualizes potential attack paths, helps identify all necessary steps for an attack, and suggests where to place countermeasures.

When and How Often to Perform Threat Modelling:

- New Applications/Major Features: Absolutely essential at the design phase.
- Significant Architectural Changes: When introducing new technologies, microservices, or external integrations.
- Periodic Review: Annually or bi-annually for critical applications, as threats and business context can change.
- After Major Incidents: To understand how a breach occurred and prevent recurrence.

Risk Prioritization:

Once threats and vulnerabilities are identified (whether through threat modelling or automated scanning), they must be prioritized. Not all vulnerabilities are created equal; their severity depends on their exploitability and, more importantly, their business impact and the compensatory controls that the business has in place already.

Risk Scoring Formula:
A common, simple approach is: Risk = Likelihood x Impact

- Likelihood: How probable is it that this vulnerability will be exploited? (Factors: exploitability, discoverability, attacker skill).
- Impact: What would be the business consequences if this vulnerability were exploited? (Factors: financial loss, data breach, reputational damage, operational disruption, compliance fines).

Prioritization Steps:

1. Assign Severity to Vulnerabilities: Based on technical characteristics (e.g., CVSS score for known CVEs or internal severity ratings for custom code flaws).

Example: Critical, High, Medium, Low, Informational.

2. Assess Business Impact: For each application and its identified vulnerabilities, understand the potential impact if exploited. This requires collaboration with business owners.

Example: An XSS vulnerability in a public-facing blog might be "Medium" impact, but the same XSS in an admin portal handling sensitive customer data might be "Critical" due to potential data theft and privilege escalation.

3. Calculate Risk Score: Combine severity/likelihood with business impact to get a comprehensive risk score.

Example Risk Matrix:

		Risk				
Likelihood/Exploitability	Rare (Low)	Info	Low	Low	Medium	Medium
	Unlikely (Med-Low)	Low	Low	Medium	Medium	High
	Possible (Medium)	Low	Medium	Medium	High	Critical
	Likely (Med-High)	Medium	Medium	High	High	Critical
	Almost Certain (High)	Medium	High	High	Critical	Critical
		Low	Medium	High	Very High	Critical
		Business Impact				

Table 14

Please note, this is a simple 5x5 risk matrix only for illustrative purposes, while readers are encouraged to evaluate their risk assessment needs critically and consider integrating alternative models that can offer more accuracy, adaptability, and contextual relevance.

How to read the table:

It helps to calculate the risk level of a security threat based on:

1. Likelihood/ Exploitability – How likely is it that this threat will happen?
2. Business Impact – If it happens, how badly does it affect the business?

You find the intersection of Likelihood and Business Impact to get the Risk Rating.

Example:

Scenario- A Web application allows attackers to perform Stored Cross-site scripting vulnerability.

For this vulnerability,

Likelihood: "Likely (Med-High)" → because the vulnerability is easy to find and exploit.

Business Impact: "High" → because attackers can access sensitive customer data.

How to find the Risk Rating:

1. Go to row "Likely (Med-High)" of **Likelihood/Exploitability.**
2. Go to column "High" of **Business Impact.**
3. The intersecting cell is: "High"

Final Risk Rating = High

4. Prioritize Remediation: Focus remediation efforts on vulnerabilities with the highest risk scores. This ensures that security resources are applied where they will have the greatest protective effect.

Example: An organization might decide to fix all "CRITICAL" risks within 7 days, "HIGH" risks within 30 days, "MEDIUM" within 90 days, and "LOW" on a best-effort basis or during planned refactoring.

By proactively performing threat modelling and adopting a structured risk prioritization framework, organizations can move beyond simply finding vulnerabilities to strategically addressing the most significant threats to their most valuable assets, ensuring that security efforts are always aligned with business priorities.

Phase 3: Automation & Scale

Having built a solid foundation and integrated security into daily development, Phase 3 focuses on optimizing the application security program for efficiency, accuracy, and broad enterprise coverage. This involves leveraging advanced automation, incorporating cutting-edge technologies like AI/ML, and ensuring the program can scale across a diverse and growing application portfolio, all while fostering continuous improvement.

4.9 Advanced Automation in Security Testing

Beyond merely integrating SAST/SCA into CI/CD, advanced automation aims to create a highly efficient and low-friction application security ecosystem. This involves orchestrating multiple tools, intelligently reducing noise, and automating remediation actions where feasible.

Key Aspects of Advanced Automation:

1. Orchestration of Security Tools:
    - Instead of running individual tools in isolation, use an orchestration layer or platform that can manage the execution, data collection, and correlation of findings from multiple SAST, DAST, SCA, and IAST tools.
    - Benefit: Provides a unified view of vulnerabilities, automates workflows (e.g., triggering a DAST scan after a successful SAST scan), and ensures consistent application of policies.

Example: A central AppSec platform might automatically trigger a DAST scan on a new staging deployment only if the SAST and SCA scans from the previous build passed with acceptable thresholds, indicating a basic level of code quality.

2. End-to-End DevSecOps Automation:

   Integrates security services seamlessly into the development workflow, ensuring that applications are delivered rapidly without compromising security. This flow of the pipeline stages and the tools involved in achieving a secure continuous integration and deployment process.

End-To-End DevSecOps Automation

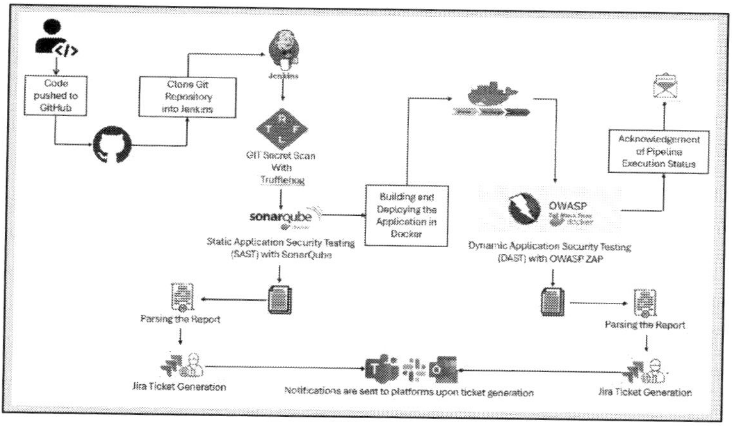

Figure 11

3. Intelligent False Positive Reduction and Triage:

   A major challenge with automated security tools is false positives. Advanced automation leverages machine learning, correlation engines, and contextual analysis to reduce this noise.

   - Techniques:

     - Baseline Management: Automatically suppress known, acceptable findings or duplicate alerts.

- Contextual Analysis: Analyse the actual exploitability of a vulnerability within the application's context (e.g., "reachability analysis" to determine if a vulnerable function is actually callable from an external entry point).
- Security Debt Management: Automatically track and categorize accepted risks or non-critical findings as "security debt" that can be addressed later.

Benefit: Developers receive fewer distracting false alarms, increasing trust in the tools and focusing on real threats.

4. Policy-as-Code for Security Gates:
   - Define security policies and compliance rules in code, allowing them to be version-controlled, tested, and automated.
   - Benefit: Ensures consistent enforcement of security policies across all pipelines and applications, promotes transparency, and simplifies auditing.

Example: A policy-as-code file might dictate: "No new critical or high-severity vulnerabilities per OWASP Top 10 are allowed in the main branch," or "All third-party libraries must not have known vulnerabilities with a CVSS score greater than 7.0."

5. Automated Remediation Actions (Limited Scope):
   - For very specific, low-risk, and well-understood vulnerabilities (e.g., misconfigurations, outdated dependencies), automation can go beyond detection to propose or even automatically implement fixes.

Example: An SCA tool might automatically create a pull request to update a vulnerable open-source library to its patched version, or a linting tool might automatically reformat code to adhere to secure coding style guidelines. This is done with caution and often requires human approval.

6. Continuous Validation of Security Controls:
   - Automate testing of security controls themselves. This ensures that implemented defences (e.g., WAF rules, authentication mechanisms) are functioning as expected and have not been bypassed by new code.

Techniques: Security regression tests, automated penetration testing tools (basic), breach and attack simulation (BAS) tools.

7. Integration with Observability and Incident Response:
   - Automate the forwarding of critical security alerts to SIEM/SOAR platforms, enabling rapid incident response.

Benefit: Reduces manual alert handling, accelerates threat detection and response, and provides richer context for security operations teams.

Advanced automation moves an organization from a reactive security posture to a proactive, self-managing, and resilient one, where security becomes a seamless, efficient, and virtually invisible part of the development and operational workflow.

4.10 AI & Machine Learning for Threat Detection

The increasing volume, velocity, and variety of data in modern application environments make manual threat detection a monumental challenge. Artificial Intelligence (AI) and Machine Learning (ML) are emerging as powerful allies in application security, offering the ability to analyse vast datasets, identify subtle anomalies, and predict potential threats with a level of precision and speed unattainable by human analysts alone.

How AI/ML Enhances Application Security:

1. Threat Detection and Prevention

- Traditional: Rule-based, Correlation engine dependent and resource-consuming.
  - ML: Using Machine Learning and Natural Language Processing to identify and prevent injection attacks in real-time. The system can be trained on massive datasets across various attack vectors, ensuring resilience against evolving threat patterns.

Example: ML models to intercept and classify inputs to evaluate legitimacy before execution, blocking harmful payloads in real time. Ideal for Injection attacks like SQL, XSS, Server-Side Template Injection, and OS Command Injections.

2. Enhanced Anomaly Detection:

- Traditional: Rule-based systems rely on predefined signatures.
- AI/ML: Can learn normal application behaviour (e.g., user login patterns, API call frequencies, database queries) and identify deviations that may indicate an attack, even without a known signature. This is crucial for detecting zero-day attacks or novel attack techniques.

Example: An ML model might detect an unusual pattern of login attempts from a new geographic location or a sudden surge in failed API calls to a specific endpoint, flagging it as suspicious behaviour rather than just a failed attempt.

3. Intelligent False Positive Reduction (Triage and Prioritization):

- One of the biggest pain points in AppSec is alert fatigue from false positives generated by traditional tools. AI/ML can be trained to distinguish between genuine vulnerabilities/attacks and benign activity.

- Technique: By analyzing historical data of true positives and false positives, ML algorithms can learn to prioritize alerts, reducing the workload on security analysts and allowing them to focus on high-fidelity threats.

Example: An AI-powered SAST tool might learn from past developer fixes to deprioritize certain code patterns that frequently appear as false positives but are benign in the context of the organization's specific codebase.

4. Predictive Analytics for Vulnerabilities:

- AI can analyse factors like code complexity, developer commit history, and past vulnerability patterns to predict which parts of an application are most likely to contain future vulnerabilities.

Benefit: Enables proactive security efforts, allowing teams to focus on manual review or more intensive testing on high-risk code segments before vulnerabilities manifest.

5. Behavioural Analytics for User and Application Entities:

- Monitoring user and application behaviour in real-time to detect anomalous activity that might indicate a compromised account or an insider threat.

Example: If an application administrator suddenly accesses sensitive data during off-hours, or makes unusual API calls they've never made before, an AI system can flag this as a potential credential compromise or insider threat.

6. Automated Vulnerability Assessment and Remediation Suggestions:

- While full automated remediation is limited, AI can analyse vulnerability reports and suggest the most likely remediation steps or even generate code snippets for common fixes.

Example: An AI system might analyse a reported XSS vulnerability and suggest sanitization functions specific to the application's framework.

Challenges and Limitations of AI/ML in AppSec:

1. Data Quality and Quantity: AI/ML models are only as good as the data they are trained on. High-quality, labelled security data is often scarce.
2. Bias: If training data is biased, the AI model can perpetuate or even amplify those biases, leading to missed threats or mis-prioritisations.
3. Explainability (Black Box Problem): Many advanced ML models operate as "black boxes," making it difficult to understand *why* a particular alert was generated or a decision was made. This can hinder trust and incident response.
4. Adversarial AI: Attackers can also use AI to craft more sophisticated, evasive attacks, leading to an AI "arms race."
5. Over-reliance: AI/ML should augment, not replace, human security expertise. Human judgment, context, and intuition remain vital for complex threats.

Despite the challenges, AI and ML are transformative technologies for application security. By intelligently processing vast amounts of security data, they enable organizations to detect threats faster, prioritize risks more effectively, and ultimately build more resilient applications at scale.

4.11 Scaling Security Across Enterprise Applications

For large organizations with hundreds or even thousands of applications, scaling application security beyond a few pilot projects presents significant challenges. This requires standardizing processes, tools, and talent, and adopting frameworks that provide centralized visibility and management of security posture across the entire application portfolio.

Key Strategies for Enterprise-Scale AppSec:

1. Centralized Governance with Federated Execution:
   - Centralized AppSec Team: A core team defines security policies, selects and manages tools, provides training, and offers expert consultation.
   - Decentralized Execution: Security activities are largely executed by individual development teams. Security champions within each team are crucial for this model.
   - Benefit: Ensures consistency and control while empowering development teams to own their security, enabling rapid execution.
2. Application Security Posture Management (ASPM) Platforms:
   - Concept: ASPM solutions aggregate findings from various AST tools (SAST, DAST, SCA, manual tests), threat intelligence, and vulnerability management systems into a single, unified view. They provide context, prioritize risks, and track remediation progress across the entire application portfolio.
   - Benefit: Solves the "alert fatigue" and "siloed data" problems, providing security and business leaders with a holistic understanding of the organization's application security risk.

Example: An ASPM dashboard might show the top 10 most vulnerable applications across the enterprise, categorized by business criticality, or track the overall MTTR for critical vulnerabilities across all development teams.

3. Standardization of Tools and Processes:
   - While some flexibility for specific tech stacks might be needed, standardize on a core set of preferred SAST, DAST, and SCA tools. This simplifies training, integration, and reporting.
   - Standardize security gates in CI/CD pipelines, secure coding guidelines, and threat modelling methodologies.
   - Benefit: Reduces complexity, increases efficiency, and ensures consistent security quality across different teams and applications.
4. Managing Legacy Applications vs. New Development:
   - New Development: Focus on "security by design" and continuous integration of security from the outset. Automated tools and secure coding practices are paramount.
   - Legacy Applications: Often harder to secure due to outdated code, lack of documentation, or specific technology constraints.
     - Strategy: Prioritize legacy apps based on business criticality and data sensitivity. Implement runtime protection (WAF, RASP). Consider phased refactoring or rewriting for the most critical and vulnerable legacy components. Regular DAST and manual penetration tests are vital.

Example: A legacy application might be too complex for SAST, but a WAF can provide a crucial layer of defence against web attacks, while regular DAST helps find runtime vulnerabilities.

5. Supply Chain Security Management:
    - As organizations rely heavily on third-party software, open-source components, and external vendors, managing this extended attack surface is critical.
    - Strategy:
        - Software Composition Analysis (SCA): Continuously monitor all open-source and third-party libraries for known vulnerabilities.
        - Software Bill of Materials (SBOM): Generate and maintain SBOMs for all applications to provide transparency into their components.
        - Vendor Risk Management: Conduct thorough security assessments of third-party vendors and their software.
        - Secure API Integrations: Ensure all third-party API integrations are securely configured and monitored.
6. Automated Security in Cloud-Native Environments:
    - Leverage cloud provider security services (e.g., AWS Security Hub, Azure Security Centre) for continuous monitoring and compliance checks.
    - Integrate security tools for serverless functions, container registries, and Kubernetes configurations into CI/CD.
    - Benefit: Takes advantage of cloud scalability and built-in security features for automated compliance and threat detection.

Scaling application security requires a strategic shift from individual efforts to a program-driven approach that is standardized, centralized in its oversight, decentralized in its execution, and continuously adapted to the diverse needs of an enterprise.

4.12 Continuous Improvement & Feedback Loops

Application security is not a destination but a continuous journey. The threat landscape, technologies, and business requirements are constantly evolving, demanding an adaptive and iterative approach to security. The final phase of the roadmap emphasizes establishing robust mechanisms for continuous improvement and feedback loops to ensure the application security program remains effective, relevant, and resilient over time.

Principles of Continuous Improvement:

1. Adaptive Security: Recognize that security posture is dynamic. What is secure today might not be secure tomorrow. Regularly review and update security policies, tools, and processes based on new threats, vulnerabilities, and technological advancements.

2. Learning from Incidents: Every security incident, near-miss, or discovered vulnerability is an opportunity to learn. Conduct "blameless post-mortems" to understand root causes, identify systemic weaknesses, and implement corrective actions that prevent recurrence.

3. Data-Driven Decisions: Rely on metrics and data (as established in 4.4 and tracked in 5.1) to assess the program's effectiveness, identify areas for improvement, and justify future investments.

4. Feedback-Oriented Culture: Foster an environment where feedback flows freely between security teams, development teams, operations, and business stakeholders.

Key Feedback Loops and Mechanisms:

1. Vulnerability Management Feedback Loop:
   - Process: Vulnerabilities identified by tools or manual tests are fed into a central tracking system (e.g., Jira). Developers remediate them. Security team re-tests and verifies fixes.
   - Improvement: Analyse trends in vulnerability types, remediation times (MTTR), and recurrence rates. If a certain vulnerability type (e.g., XSS) is consistently reappearing, it indicates a need for more targeted developer training or updated secure coding guidelines.

Example: If SAST keeps flagging the same insecure pattern in new code, the security team might schedule a specific training session for the affected teams or update the IDE plugin to provide better inline warnings.

2. Developer Feedback on Tools and Processes:
   - Process: Regularly solicit feedback from developers on the usability, accuracy, and performance of security tools and processes.
   - Improvement: Use this feedback to tune tools, reduce false positives, improve integration, and make security processes less burdensome. If developers complain about slow SAST scans, investigate faster alternatives or optimize current configurations.

Example: Conducting quarterly surveys or informal "coffee connect" sessions with developers to gather their input on what's working and what's not.

3. Security Champions Feedback:
   - Process: The security champions network serves as a vital conduit for feedback from development teams to the central security team and vice versa.

- Improvement: Champions can highlight common challenges, suggest improvements to tools or training, and flag emerging security concerns from their teams. They also help disseminate new security practices.

4. Incident Response Lessons Learned:
   - Process: After every security incident (minor or major), conduct a thorough post-mortem analysis. Document what happened, why it happened, what was done effectively, and what could be improved.
   - Improvement: Use these lessons to update threat models, enhance security controls, refine incident response playbooks, and inform future secure design decisions.

Example: If a breach occurred due to an unpatched vulnerability in a web server, the lesson learned might be to implement more stringent patch management processes for all internet-facing infrastructure and integrate automated vulnerability scanning for server configurations into deployment pipelines.

5. Threat Intelligence Integration:
   - Process: Continuously monitor the external threat landscape, new attack techniques, and emerging vulnerabilities (e.g., from CISA alerts, security research, industry reports).
   - Improvement: Use this intelligence to proactively update threat models, adjust security controls, and inform developer training on emerging risks.

Example: If a new critical vulnerability is discovered in a widely used web framework, the security team can immediately push out an alert to affected development teams, prioritize patches, and update relevant security scanning rules.

6. Regulatory and Compliance Updates:
    - Process: Stay abreast of changes in data privacy laws and industry standards.
    - Improvement: Adjust security policies, controls, and testing methodologies to maintain compliance and avoid fines.

By embedding continuous improvement and feedback loops into the application security program, an organization ensures that its security posture remains robust, adaptable, and aligned with the dynamic demands of the digital world. Security becomes a living, evolving capability that learns and grows with the business.

Chapter 5: Key Metrics to Measure Success

Establishing a vision and executing a roadmap for application security, as outlined in the previous chapters, are crucial steps. However, without a robust framework for measuring success, these efforts can lose direction, fail to demonstrate value, and struggle to secure continued investment. This chapter focuses on the essential metrics that organizations must track to understand the effectiveness of their application security program, identify areas for improvement, and communicate tangible results to all stakeholders. Effective metrics translate technical achievements into business language, proving that security is not just a cost, but a critical enabler of business resilience and growth.

5.1 Vulnerability Detection & Remediation Rates

At the heart of any application security program lies the ability to find and fix vulnerabilities. Therefore, measuring the efficiency of both detection and remediation is fundamental. These metrics provide a direct indication of how well an organization is identifying security flaws and how quickly it is addressing them, directly impacting its overall risk posture.

Vulnerability Detection Rate

The vulnerability detection rate quantifies how effectively an organization's security testing tools and processes are identifying security weaknesses within its applications. It's not just about the raw number of vulnerabilities, but often about the *rate* at which new ones are discovered or the *proportion* of high-severity flaws found.

Definition:

There are several ways to define "detection rate" depending on what aspect is being measured:

- Raw Number of New Vulnerabilities: The total count of unique vulnerabilities discovered over a specific period (e.g., per sprint, per month, per quarter). This is a simple starting point.
- Vulnerability Density: The number of vulnerabilities per unit of code (e.g., per 1,000 lines of code (KLOC) or per application). This normalizes the count, making it comparable across different application sizes or teams.

Formula: Vulnerability Density = (Total Vulnerabilities / Total Lines of Code) * 1000

- Percentage of Applications Scanned/Tested with Findings: The proportion of applications (especially critical ones) that, when tested, yield security findings. This indicates the effectiveness of the scanning/testing program in uncovering issues.
- Unique Vulnerabilities Found by New Methods/Tools: Tracking vulnerabilities found specifically by newly introduced tools or processes (e.g., threat modelling, new SAST rules or a new security testing tool created internally).

Importance:

- Identifies Security Debt: A high detection rate, especially for critical vulnerabilities, indicates significant existing and mounting security debt that needs addressing.
- Validates Testing Efficacy: Shows that security testing tools and processes are actively working and configured correctly.

- Informs Prioritization: Helps identify which applications or codebases are most prone to vulnerabilities, guiding where to focus remediation efforts or developer training.

Example Calculation & Tracking:

Consider a new feature for an online banking application developed over a quarter.

- Total lines of new code: 10,000
- SAST findings (critical/high): 20
- DAST findings (critical/high in staging): 5
- Manual review findings (critical/high): 2

Total critical/high vulnerabilities detected: 27

Vulnerability Density (SAST): (20 / 10,000) * 1000 = 2 vulnerabilities per KLOC

Over time, you would want to see the critical/high vulnerabilities decrease, indicating successful "shift-left" practices. However, the *absolute number* of detected vulnerabilities might initially rise as new tools are implemented and coverage increases, which is a sign of improved visibility, not necessarily worse security.

Remediation Rate

The remediation rate measures the effectiveness and speed with which discovered vulnerabilities are fixed and verified. It's crucial because detecting vulnerabilities is only half the battle; they must be resolved to reduce actual risk.

Definition:

- Number of Vulnerabilities Remediated: The count of unique vulnerabilities that have been fixed and verified over a specific period.

- Percentage of Vulnerabilities Remediated: The proportion of detected vulnerabilities that have been successfully resolved within a given timeframe.
  - Formula: Percentage Remediated = (Number of Vulnerabilities Fixed / Total Number of Vulnerabilities Discovered) * 100%
- Backlog Growth/Reduction: Tracking the net change in the total number of open vulnerabilities over time. A shrinking backlog indicates effective remediation.
- Remediation Compliance: The percentage of vulnerabilities fixed within their defined Service Level Agreements (SLAs) or target remediation times (e.g., critical bugs fixed within 5days).

Importance:

- Direct Risk Reduction: Shows that security findings are being acted upon and that the organization's attack surface is shrinking.
- Efficiency of Development/Security Teams: Reflects the ability of development and security teams to collaborate and efficiently address security debt.
- Compliance Demonstration: Essential for demonstrating due diligence to auditors and regulators.

Example Calculation & Tracking:

Continuing the example from above, suppose over the next month:

- Total critical/high vulnerabilities detected in Q1: 27
- Vulnerabilities fixed and verified in April: 15
- New critical/high vulnerabilities found in April: 8

Tracking Table for Vulnerability Management (Quarterly Snapshot):

Metric	Q1 2025	Q2 2025	Q3 2025	Q4 2025
New Critical/High Vulns Detected	27	20	18	15
Total Critical/High Vulns Fixed	15	22	25	20
Remediation Rate (Qtr)	42.8%	110% (can exceed if fixing backlog)	138%	100%
Vulnerability Backlog (End of Qtr)	12 (27-15)	10 (12+20-22)	3 (10+18-25)	-2 (3+15-20)
Avg. Vulnerability Density (per KLOC)	2.0	1.8	1.5	1.2

Table 15

Remediation Rate (April): (15 / (27 (from Q1) + 8 (new in April))) * 100% = (15 / 35) * 100% = 42.8%

Backlog Calculation for Q1 = No initial backlog, hence vulnerabilities detected – vulnerabilities fixed (27 – 15 = 12)

Backlog Calculation for Q2 = Previous Backlog + vulnerabilities detected – vulnerabilities fixed (12+20-22 = 10)

Backlog Calculation for Q3 = Previous Backlog + vulnerabilities detected – vulnerabilities fixed (10+18-25 = 3)

Backlog Calculation for Q4 = Previous Backlog + vulnerabilities detected – vulnerabilities fixed (3+15-20 = -2)

The goal for remediation rates should ideally be 100% or more, meaning you're fixing all newly found vulnerabilities *and* reducing the backlog. Consistent improvement in these rates indicates a maturing application security program.

5.2 Mean Time to Detect (MTTD)

Definition: MTTD is the average time it takes for an organization to identify a security vulnerability or incident from the moment it occurs or is introduced into the system.

While detection and remediation rates focus on the quantity of vulnerabilities, Mean Time to Detect (MTTD) introduces the crucial element of speed. It reflects how quickly an organization can identify a security event or vulnerability and subsequently neutralize the threat.

Components of MTTD:

- Time to Introduction: When a vulnerability is first introduced into the codebase or system (e.g., a developer commits insecure code, a misconfiguration is deployed).

- Time to Discovery: When the vulnerability is first identified by a tool, process, or individual (e.g., SAST scan, DAST scan, manual review, penetration test, security researcher report, or a real-world attack).

Formula: MTTD = (Sum of [Time of Discovery - Time of Introduction/Occurrence] for all vulnerabilities/incidents) / Total Number of Vulnerabilities/Incidents

- Practical Calculation: Often, "Time of Introduction" is hard to pinpoint precisely for every vulnerability. Therefore, in practice, MTTD is often calculated as (Time of Discovery - Time of Last Known Secure State / Time of Previous Scan). For new code, it's simpler: (Time of Scan Detection - Time of Code Commit).

Importance:

- Early Detection is Key: A lower MTTD means vulnerabilities are found closer to their point of introduction or occurrence. This is a direct measure of "shifting left."
- Reduced Exposure Window: The shorter the time a vulnerability remains undetected, the less opportunity an attacker has to discover and exploit it.
- Cost Efficiency: As noted in Chapter 4, the cost of fixing a vulnerability increases dramatically the later it is found. A low MTTD translates directly to significant cost savings.
- Operational Awareness: Indicates how well an organization's monitoring, logging, and security testing mechanisms are performing in real-time or near real-time.

Example:

- Scenario 1 (Traditional): A critical vulnerability is introduced in an application in January. It's only found during a quarterly penetration test in March. MTTD = ~60 days.
- Scenario 2 (Shift-Left): A critical vulnerability is introduced in a code commit at 9:00 AM. An automated SAST scan in the CI/CD pipeline identifies it at 9:05 AM. MTTD = 5 minutes.

Organizations should strive for a low MTTD, especially for critical applications. This often means investing in continuous, automated security testing integrated directly into developer workflows and CI/CD pipelines, and robust real-time monitoring in production.

Tracking MTTD (Overall Program Performance):

Metric	Baseline (Q1 2025)	Target (Q1 2026)	Target (Q1 2027)
Avg. MTTD (Critical/High Vulns)	60 days	15 days	7 days

Table 16

These metrics should be tracked separately for different severity levels (Critical, High, Medium, Low) and potentially by different discovery methods (e.g., MTTD for SAST vs. MTTD for penetration tests) to gain granular insights. A continuous focus on lowering MTTD demonstrates a mature, agile, and effective application security program.

5.3 Test Coverage & Compliance Adherence

Beyond simply finding and fixing vulnerabilities, a robust application security program must also ensure comprehensive test coverage and demonstrable adherence to relevant compliance standards. These metrics indicate the breadth and depth of security efforts, assuring stakeholders that critical areas are not being overlooked and that legal and regulatory obligations are being met.

Test Coverage

Test coverage in application security refers to the extent to which security testing activities cover the application's code, functionalities, attack surface, and deployment environment.

It's about minimizing blind spots and ensuring that all critical components are subjected to appropriate security scrutiny.

Definition & Measurement:

- Code Coverage by SAST: The percentage of an application's source code analysed by SAST tools. While 100% code coverage does not guarantee 100% vulnerability detection, it ensures that no part of the code is entirely ignored.

Formula: (Lines of Code Scanned by SAST / Total Lines of Code) * 100%

- Application Coverage by DAST/Pentest: The percentage of critical or high-risk applications that undergo regular DAST scans or manual penetration tests.

Formula: (Number of Critical/High Apps Scanned by DAST / Total Critical/High Apps) * 100%

- Attack Surface Coverage (Threat Modelling): The extent to which critical data flows, external interfaces (APIs, web UIs), and trust boundaries have been subjected to threat modelling. This is often qualitative initially but can evolve to track coverage of specific architectural components.
    - Measurement: Percentage of critical APIs/microservices/external integrations that have undergone formal threat modelling.
    - Another method of calculating attack surface (manual testing) is to decompose the application into individual modules/functionalities and map applicable tests from OWASP to these individual functionalities (providing a test coverage spreadsheet snapshot as example)

OWASP Top 10

S. No	Module	Subset	Broken Access Control			Cryptographic Failures			Injection			Insecure Design			Security Misconfiguration		
			Applicable	Test Status	Vulnerability	Applicable	Test Status	Vulnerability	Applicable	Test Status	Vulnerability	Applicable	Test Status	Vulnerability	Applicable	Test Status	Vulnerability
1	Login page	Login	Yes	Executed	Confirmed	Yes	Executed	Confirmed	Yes	Executed	No Issues	Yes	Executed	No Issues	Yes	Executed	Confirmed
		signup	Yes	Executed	Confirmed	Yes	Executed	Confirmed	Yes	Executed	No Issues	Yes	Executed	No Issues	Yes	Executed	Confirmed
		forgot password	Yes	Executed	Confirmed	Yes	Executed	Confirmed	Yes	Executed	No Issues	Yes	Executed	No Issues	Yes	Executed	Confirmed
2	Account Setup	Billing	Yes	Executed	Confirmed	Yes	Executed	Confirmed	Yes	Executed	No Issues	Yes	Executed	No Issues	Yes	Executed	Confirmed
		Settings	Yes	Executed	Confirmed	Yes	Executed	Confirmed	No	Not Applicable		Yes	Executed	No Issues	Yes	Executed	Confirmed
		Page Code Builder	Yes	Executed	Confirmed	Yes	Executed	Confirmed	No	Not Applicable		Yes	Executed	No Issues	Yes	Executed	Confirmed
		Collaboration	Yes	Executed	Confirmed	Yes	Executed	Confirmed	No	Not Applicable		Yes	Executed	No Issues	Yes	Executed	Confirmed
		Online Status	Yes	Executed	Confirmed	Yes	Executed	Confirmed	No	Not Applicable		Yes	Executed	No Issues	Yes	Executed	Confirmed
		Visitor Policies	Yes	Executed	No Issues	Yes	Executed	Confirmed	Yes	Not Applicable		Yes	Executed	No Issues	Yes	Executed	Confirmed
		Applications	Yes	Executed	Confirmed	Yes	Executed	Confirmed	No	Not Applicable		Yes	Executed	No Issues	Yes	Executed	Confirmed
3	Delivery	CNPS Management	Yes	Executed	Confirmed	Yes	Executed	Confirmed	Yes	Executed	No Issues	Yes	Executed	No Issues	Yes	Executed	Confirmed
		PCI Management	Yes	Executed	Confirmed	Yes	Executed	Confirmed	Yes	Executed	No Issues	Yes	Executed	No Issues	Yes	Executed	Confirmed
		CNPS	Yes	Executed	Confirmed	Yes	Executed	Confirmed	No	Not Applicable		Yes	Executed	No Issues	Yes	Executed	Confirmed
		QBR & MBR	Yes	Executed	Confirmed	Yes	Executed	Confirmed	Yes	Executed	No Issues	Yes	Executed	No Issues	Yes	Executed	Confirmed
4	Operations	Employee Details	Yes	Executed	Confirmed	Yes	Executed	Confirmed	No	Not Applicable		Yes	Executed	No Issues	Yes	Executed	Confirmed
		Allocation Details	Yes	Executed	Confirmed	Yes	Executed	Confirmed	Yes	Executed	No Issues	Yes	Executed	No Issues	Yes	Executed	Confirmed
		Demand Overdue	Yes	Executed	Confirmed	Yes	Executed	Confirmed	No	Not Applicable		Yes	Executed	No Issues	Yes	Executed	Confirmed
		Utilization Forecast	Yes	Executed	Confirmed	Yes	Executed	Confirmed	No	Not Applicable		Yes	Executed	No Issues	Yes	Executed	Confirmed
5	People	ENPS Management	Yes	Executed	Confirmed	Yes	Executed	Confirmed	Yes	Executed	No Issues	Yes	Executed	No Issues	Yes	Executed	Confirmed
		Attrition Management	Yes	Executed	Confirmed	Yes	Executed	Confirmed	Yes	Executed	No Issues	Yes	Executed	No Issues	Yes	Executed	Confirmed
		ENPS & Hiring Statistics	Yes	Executed	Confirmed	Yes	Executed	Confirmed	No	Not Applicable		Yes	Executed	No Issues	Yes	Executed	Confirmed
		Talent Acquisition	Yes	Executed	Confirmed	Yes	Executed	Confirmed	No	Not Applicable		Yes	Executed	No Issues	Yes	Executed	Confirmed
		Monthly Global Joiners	Yes	Executed	Confirmed	Yes	Executed	Confirmed	No	Not Applicable		Yes	Executed	No Issues	Yes	Executed	Confirmed
		Allocation History	Yes	Executed	Confirmed	Yes	Executed	Confirmed	Yes	Executed	No Issues	Yes	Executed	No Issues	Yes	Executed	Confirmed
6	Resource Management	Resource Requisition Summary	Yes	Executed	Confirmed	Yes	Executed	Confirmed	No	Not Applicable		Yes	Executed	No Issues	Yes	Executed	Confirmed
7	Hiring Management	Hiring Requests	Yes	Executed	Confirmed	Yes	Executed	Confirmed	Yes	Executed	No Issues	Yes	Executed	No Issues	Yes	Executed	Confirmed
8	Skills	My Skills	Yes	Executed	Confirmed	Yes	Executed	Confirmed	Yes	Executed	No Issues	Yes	Executed	No Issues	Yes	Executed	Confirmed

* Yes Indicates Test is Applicable
* NA Indicates Test is Not Applicable

OWASP Top 10

S. No	Module	Subset	Vulnerable and Outdated			Identification and Authentication			Software and Data Integrity			Security Logging and Monitoring			Server-Side Request Forgery (SSRF)		
			Applicable	Test Status	Vulnerability	Applicable	Test Status	Vulnerability	Applicable	Test Status	Vulnerability	Applicable	Test Status	Vulnerability	Applicable	Test Status	Vulnerability
1	Login page	Login	Yes	Executed	Confirmed	Yes	Executed	Confirmed	Yes	Executed	Confirmed	No	Not Applicable		No	Not Applicable	
		signup	Yes	Executed	Confirmed	Yes	Executed	Confirmed	Yes	Executed	Confirmed	No	Not Applicable		No	Not Applicable	
		forgot password	Yes	Executed	Confirmed	Yes	Executed	Confirmed	Yes	Executed	Confirmed	No	Not Applicable		No	Not Applicable	
2	Account Setup	Billing	Yes	Executed	Confirmed	Yes	Executed	Confirmed	Yes	Executed	Confirmed	No	Not Applicable		No	Not Applicable	
		Settings	Yes	Executed	Confirmed	Yes	Executed	Confirmed	Yes	Executed	Confirmed	No	Not Applicable		No	Not Applicable	
		Page Code Builder	Yes	Executed	Confirmed	Yes	Executed	Confirmed	Yes	Executed	Confirmed	No	Not Applicable		No	Not Applicable	
		Collaboration	Yes	Executed	Confirmed	Yes	Executed	Confirmed	Yes	Executed	Confirmed	No	Not Applicable		No	Not Applicable	
		Online Status	Yes	Executed	Confirmed	Yes	Executed	Confirmed	Yes	Executed	Confirmed	No	Not Applicable		No	Not Applicable	
		Visitor Policies	Yes	Executed	Confirmed	Yes	Executed	Confirmed	Yes	Executed	Confirmed	No	Not Applicable		No	Not Applicable	
		Applications	Yes	Executed	Confirmed	Yes	Executed	Confirmed	Yes	Executed	Confirmed	No	Not Applicable		No	Not Applicable	
3	Delivery	CNPS Management	Yes	Executed	Confirmed	Yes	Executed	Confirmed	Yes	Executed	Confirmed	No	Not Applicable		No	Not Applicable	
		PCI Management	Yes	Executed	Confirmed	Yes	Executed	Confirmed	Yes	Executed	Confirmed	No	Not Applicable		No	Not Applicable	
		CNPS	Yes	Executed	Confirmed	Yes	Executed	Confirmed	Yes	Executed	Confirmed	No	Not Applicable		No	Not Applicable	
		QBR & MBR	Yes	Executed	Confirmed	Yes	Executed	Confirmed	Yes	Executed	Confirmed	No	Not Applicable		No	Not Applicable	
4	Operations	Employee Details	Yes	Executed	Confirmed	Yes	Executed	Confirmed	Yes	Executed	Confirmed	No	Not Applicable		No	Not Applicable	
		Allocation Details	Yes	Executed	Confirmed	Yes	Executed	Confirmed	Yes	Executed	Confirmed	No	Not Applicable		No	Not Applicable	
		Demand Overdue	Yes	Executed	Confirmed	Yes	Executed	Confirmed	Yes	Executed	Confirmed	No	Not Applicable		No	Not Applicable	
		Utilization Forecast	Yes	Executed	Confirmed	Yes	Executed	Confirmed	Yes	Executed	Confirmed	No	Not Applicable		No	Not Applicable	
5	People	ENPS Management	Yes	Executed	Confirmed	Yes	Executed	Confirmed	Yes	Executed	Confirmed	No	Not Applicable		No	Not Applicable	
		Attrition Management	Yes	Executed	Confirmed	Yes	Executed	Confirmed	Yes	Executed	Confirmed	No	Not Applicable		No	Not Applicable	
		ENPS & Hiring Statistics	Yes	Executed	Confirmed	Yes	Executed	Confirmed	Yes	Executed	Confirmed	No	Not Applicable		No	Not Applicable	
		Talent Acquisition	Yes	Executed	Confirmed	Yes	Executed	Confirmed	Yes	Executed	Confirmed	No	Not Applicable		No	Not Applicable	
		Monthly Global Joiners	Yes	Executed	Confirmed	Yes	Executed	Confirmed	Yes	Executed	Confirmed	No	Not Applicable		No	Not Applicable	
		Allocation History	Yes	Executed	Confirmed	Yes	Executed	Confirmed	Yes	Executed	Confirmed	No	Not Applicable		No	Not Applicable	
6	Resource Management	Resource Requisition Summary	Yes	Executed	Confirmed	Yes	Executed	Confirmed	Yes	Executed	Confirmed	No	Not Applicable		No	Not Applicable	
7	Hiring Management	Hiring Requests	Yes	Executed	Confirmed	Yes	Executed	Confirmed	Yes	Executed	Confirmed	No	Not Applicable		No	Not Applicable	
8	Skills	My Skills	Yes	Executed	Confirmed	Yes	Executed	Confirmed	Yes	Executed	Confirmed	No	Not Applicable		Yes	Executed	No Issues

* Yes Indicates Test is Applicable
* NA Indicates Test is Not Applicable

This Test coverage sheet provides a detailed mapping of target application modules against the OWASP Top 10 security vulnerabilities. It provides information about the applicability of each vulnerability type to specific features, along with their testing status and results. The document ensures thorough security assessment coverage and highlights confirmed vulnerabilities for further action.

To download sample test coverage sheet (soft copies) email us @ **appsecbook.templates@gmail.com** with the serial number of the book.

- Third-Party Component Coverage (SCA): The percentage of an application's third-party and open-source dependencies that are regularly scanned by an SCA tool.

Formula: (Number of Detected Dependencies Scanned by SCA / Total Number of Dependencies) * 100%

- Security Control Coverage: The percentage of defined security controls (e.g., authentication, authorization, input validation) that are covered by automated unit/integration tests or manual test cases.

Importance:

- Reduces Blind Spots: Ensures that security efforts are comprehensive and not just focused on easily found vulnerabilities.
- Minimizes Unknown Risks: Helps uncover vulnerabilities in less-travelled code paths or newly introduced components.
- Informs Resource Allocation: Identifies areas where more testing or different testing methodologies are needed.

- Builds Confidence: Assures leadership and compliance teams that the security program is thorough.

Example Tracking for Test Coverage (Quarterly):

Metric	Q1 2025	Q2 2025	Q3 2025	Q4 2025
SAST Code Coverage (Avg. per critical app)	65%	70%	75%	80%
% Critical Apps with DAST/Pentest	20%	30%	40%	50%
% New Features/Major Changes with Threat Modelling	10%	25%	40%	60%
SCA Coverage of Dependencies	80%	85%	90%	95%

Table 17

Compliance Adherence

Compliance adherence measures the extent to which an organization's application security practices, controls, and documentation meet the requirements of relevant regulatory standards (e.g., GDPR, HIPAA, PCI DSS, SOX) and internal policies. This is crucial for avoiding legal penalties, demonstrating due diligence, and maintaining licenses to operate in certain sectors.

Definition & Measurement:

- Policy Compliance Rate: The percentage of security policies and secure coding guidelines that are demonstrably implemented and followed within application development.

- Measurement: Audit findings, automated policy checks (e.g., via static analysis rulesets), developer adherence scores.

  - Regulatory Requirement Fulfilment: For specific regulations, track the completion rate of required security controls or assessments.

Example (PCI DSS): Percentage of in-scope public-facing web applications protected by WAFs; percentage of annual penetration tests completed for cardholder data environments.

Example (GDPR): Number of Data Protection Impact Assessments (DPIAs) completed for new features handling personal data; documented implementation of "privacy by design" principles.

  - Audit Readiness Score: A qualitative or quantitative score indicating how prepared the organization is for external security and compliance audits. This is often based on the completeness and accuracy of documentation, evidence of controls, and successful internal audits.

  - Number of Compliance Violations/Audit Findings: Tracking the reduction in findings from internal or external compliance audits related to application security.

Importance:

  - Legal & Financial Risk Mitigation: Directly reduces the risk of fines, legal actions, and business restrictions.

  - Trust and Reputation: Demonstrates a commitment to protecting sensitive data, which is vital for customer and partner trust.

- Market Access: Compliance is often a prerequisite for operating in certain industries or geographic regions.
- Good Governance: Ensures that security practices are aligned with the organization's legal and ethical obligations.

Example Tracking for Compliance Adherence (Annual/Bi-annual):

Compliance Domain	Baseline (2024)	Target (2025)	Target (2026)
PCI DSS - Req. 6.4.2 (WAF for public apps)	70%	90%	100%
GDPR - New DPIAs for high-risk data processing	50%	80%	100%
SOX - Apps processing financial data with access controls audited	85%	95%	100%
Internal Secure Coding Policy Adherence	60%	75%	90%
Number of Critical Compliance Findings (Audit)	5	2	0

Table 18

By consistently monitoring test coverage and compliance adherence, organizations can ensure that their application security efforts are not only effective in finding and fixing vulnerabilities but also comprehensive in scope and fully compliant with necessary regulations, building a foundation of trust and accountability.

5.4 ROI of Security Testing Initiatives

Security is often perceived as a cost centre, but a mature application security program is a strategic investment with a demonstrable Return on Investment (ROI). Quantifying the ROI of security testing initiatives is crucial for justifying budget allocation, securing executive buy-in, and integrating security into broader business strategy. ROI moves the conversation from fear-based spending to value-driven investment.

Defining ROI for Application Security:
ROI in security can be both quantitative (measurable financial impact) and qualitative (non-financial benefits that contribute to business value).

Quantitative ROI:
This focuses on measurable cost savings and avoided losses.

Avoided Breach Costs:

- Concept: The most significant financial benefit of effective security is preventing data breaches. Calculating the potential cost of a breach and demonstrating how security investments reduce this likelihood contributes directly to ROI.

- Measurement:
    - Research the average cost of data breaches in your industry (e.g., from IBM's Cost of a Data Breach Report).
    - Estimate the likelihood of a breach occurring without specific security initiatives.
    - Attribute a reduction in likelihood (or potential impact) from the security testing initiatives.
    - Avoided Cost = (Estimated Breach Cost * Reduction in Breach Probability)

Example: If a potential breach could cost $5 million, and a robust AppSec program is estimated to reduce the probability of such a breach by 20%, the avoided cost is $1 million ($5,000,000 * 0.20). If the security program costs $200,000, the ROI is significant.

2. Reduced Cost of Vulnerability Remediation ("Shift Left" Savings):

    - Concept: Fixing vulnerabilities early in the SDLC is significantly cheaper than fixing them late. Security testing initiatives (especially SAST, SCA, threat modelling) enable this "shift left."

    - Measurement: Track the average cost of fixing vulnerabilities at different stages (e.g., design, coding, testing, production). Compare the number of vulnerabilities found and fixed early vs. late.

Example:

- Cost to fix a bug in design: $100
- Cost to fix a bug in coding: $1,000
- Cost to fix a bug in testing: $10,000
- Cost to fix a bug in production: $100,000
- If a SAST tool (costing $X) helps detect 50 bugs in the coding phase that would have otherwise reached production, saving $100,000 - $1,000 = $99,000 per bug, the total savings are substantial.

Efficiency Gains / Accelerated Time-to-Market:

- Concept: Automated security testing in CI/CD pipelines can reduce the time and effort spent on manual security reviews and re-work, thus accelerating release cycles.

- Measurement:
    - Reduction in Mean Time to Release.

- Reduction in security-related delays for application releases.
- Savings in the security team's manual review hours.

Example: If automated security gates save 2 weeks of manual security review and re-testing per major release, and there are 10 major releases annually, this translates to 20 weeks of saved development/security team time, which can be quantified in terms of salaries or faster product delivery to market.

Reduced Compliance Fines and Penalties:

- Concept: Proactive application security helps meet regulatory requirements, avoiding substantial fines.
- Measurement: Track the number and value of avoided fines due to adherence to regulations (e.g., GDPR, HIPAA, PCI DSS).

Example: Avoiding a GDPR fine of up to €20 million or 4% of global turnover is a direct ROI from investing in GDPR-compliant application security practices.

Qualitative ROI:

These are non-financial benefits that, while harder to quantify directly, contribute significantly to the organization's long-term value and competitive position.

1. Enhanced Brand Reputation and Customer Trust:
    - Concept: A strong security posture builds trust with customers, partners, and the market. A reputation for security can differentiate an organization from competitors.
    - Measurement (Indirect): Customer satisfaction scores related to security, positive media mentions, reduction in customer complaints about data privacy, analyst ratings.

Example: A transparent security program leads to positive customer testimonials, increasing customer acquisition and retention rates.

2. Improved Developer Productivity and Morale:
   - Concept: When security is integrated and seamless, developers feel empowered, not burdened. Clear guidelines and helpful tools improve their efficiency and job satisfaction.
   - Measurement (Indirect): Developer surveys, reduction in developer frustration related to security, improved team collaboration.
3. Competitive Advantage:
   - Concept: Being demonstrably more secure can attract clients in highly regulated industries or those with strong security requirements.
   - Measurement (Indirect): Winning new contracts based on security maturity, ability to enter new security-sensitive markets, and higher market valuation.
4. Better Decision-Making and Risk Management:
   - Concept: Accurate security metrics and visibility allow for better risk prioritization and strategic decision-making.
   - Measurement (Indirect): Reduced number of high-impact incidents, more efficient resource allocation, clearer communication of risk to the board.

Calculating Overall ROI:

A simplified ROI formula:

ROI = (Total Benefit - Total Cost) / Total Cost

Where:

- Total Benefit: Sum of all quantifiable avoided costs (breach, remediation, fines) and efficiency gains.
- Total Cost: Sum of all security program expenses (tools, training, personnel, consulting).

Example ROI Statement for a Board Presentation:
"By investing $500,000 in our new application security automation platform and developer training program this year, we have already achieved estimated avoided breach costs of $1.5 million, reduced remediation expenses by $750,000 by shifting left, and accelerated release cycles by an average of 3 days per sprint. This represents a preliminary ROI of over 450% and a significant enhancement to our brand reputation and compliance standing, positioning us as a leader in secure software delivery."

By consistently measuring and communicating these quantitative and qualitative benefits, application security leaders can transform security from a cost centre into a strategic asset that demonstrably contributes to the organization's bottom line and long-term success.

We can also create a simple security testing measurement framework to establish a systematic approach for evaluating and reporting the effectiveness and efficiencies of security testing. This framework aims to provide quantitative and qualitative insights into the security posture of the system under test.

The security testing measurements framework's main goal is to help testing teams gather and analyse important metrics about their target. It organizes information collected during testing, making data collection more efficient and effective. The following image depicts various measures and metrics that can be captured and reported as part of security testing.

Figure 12

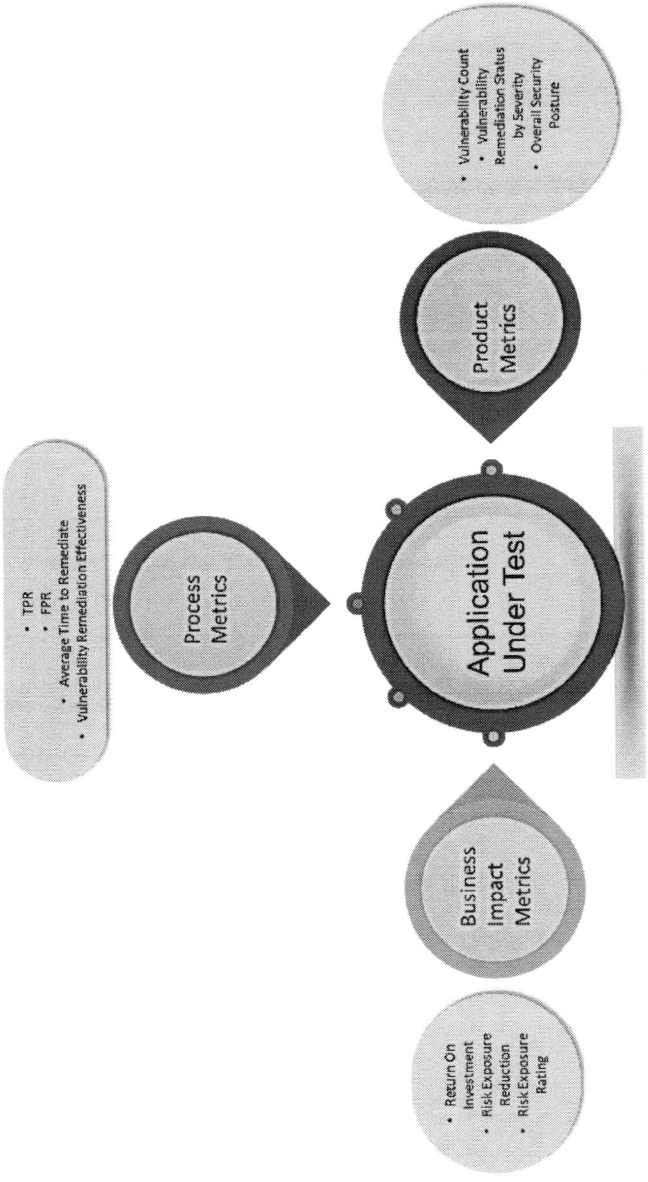
Application Under Test
Process Metrics
• TPR
• FPR
• Average Time to Remediate
• Vulnerability Remediation Effectiveness
Product Metrics
• Vulnerability Count
• Vulnerability Remediation Status by Severity
• Overall Security Posture
Business Impact Metrics
• Return On Investment
• Risk Exposure Reduction
• Risk Exposure Rating

Chapter – 6: Business Impact

In the preceding chapters, we have explored the strategic importance of application security, defined a clear vision, and outlined a comprehensive roadmap for its implementation. However, the true measure of any enterprise-wide initiative lies in its demonstrable contribution to the core business. This chapter shifts the focus from the "how" to the "why," detailing the profound and multifaceted business impact that a mature application security program delivers. Far from being a mere cost centre or an inconvenient obligation, application security, when strategically implemented, becomes a powerful enabler of growth, a protector of value, and a significant competitive differentiator.

6.1 Cost Savings from Proactive Security

One of the most compelling arguments for investing in robust application security is the substantial cost savings it generates. While security spending might initially appear as an overhead, a proactive, "shift-left" approach demonstrably reduces expenses across various operational domains, ultimately contributing to a healthier bottom line. These savings are realized from preventing costly incidents, optimizing development workflows, and avoiding significant financial penalties.

1. Reduced Cost of Vulnerability Remediation

The principle of "shifting left" security activities—identifying and addressing vulnerabilities as early as possible in the software development lifecycle (SDLC)—is the single most impactful driver of cost savings in application security. The cost of fixing a bug escalates dramatically the later it is discovered.

- Illustrative Cost Escalation:
  - Requirements/Design Phase: Fixing a security flaw at this stage might involve a simple change to a document or an architectural diagram. The cost is minimal, perhaps a few hours of an architect's time (e.g., $100).
  - Coding Phase: A developer fixes a bug identified by an IDE plugin or a SAST tool as they write the code. This might take a few hours (e.g., $1,000).
  - Testing Phase: A bug discovered during QA or DAST scanning requires developers to switch context, fix the code, re-test, and potentially re-deploy to a staging environment. This involves multiple teams and processes (e.g., $10,000).
  - Production Phase: A critical vulnerability discovered in a live application often necessitates immediate attention, emergency patches, potential downtime, and extensive re-testing. The cost spirals (e.g., $100,000+).

Example:

Consider an organization that historically found 20 critical vulnerabilities in production applications annually. If each of these costs an average of $100,000 to remediate in production, the total annual cost for fixing these critical bugs alone would be $2 million. By implementing a "shift-left" strategy through integrated SAST and developer training (costing, for instance, $300,000 per year), the organization might now catch 80% of these critical flaws in the coding phase.

- Before Shift-Left: 20 critical vulnerabilities in production = $2,000,000
- After Shift-Left:
  - 16 critical vulnerabilities caught in coding (80% of 20) = 16 * $1,000 = $16,000

  - 4 critical vulnerabilities still reach production (20% of 20) = 4 * $100,000 = $400,000
  - Total remediation cost = $416,000
- Annual Savings: $2,000,000 - $416,000 = $1,584,000

This direct cost reduction in remediation alone can often justify a significant portion of an application security program's budget.

2. Avoided Costs of Security Incidents and Data Breaches

The most catastrophic financial impacts often stem from full-blown security incidents and data breaches. Proactive security testing is designed to prevent these events, leading to massive avoided costs.

- Direct Costs of a Breach: These include incident response (forensics, containment), legal fees, regulatory fines (as discussed in 6.3), customer notification costs, public relations expenses, and the cost of providing identity theft protection or credit monitoring services.

- Indirect Costs of a Breach: This encompasses loss of customer trust and churn, reputational damage, increased insurance premiums, lost revenue due to downtime, intellectual property theft, and potential devaluation of the company.

According to IBM's "Cost of a Data Breach Report 2024," the global average cost of a data breach reached $4.88 million. For industries handling highly sensitive data, like healthcare, this average can be significantly higher. By investing in comprehensive application security testing (SAST, DAST, SCA, penetration testing, threat modelling), organizations reduce the likelihood of such costly events, directly translating to avoided expenses.

Example: An organization invests $1 million in an advanced AppSec program. If this program demonstrably reduces the probability of a $5 million data breach by 30%, the avoided cost is $1.5 million (\$5,000,000 * 0.30). This single avoided breach can pay for the security program many times over.

3. Increased Operational Efficiency and Faster Development Cycles

Paradoxically, robust application security can actually accelerate development and improve operational efficiency.

- Reduced Rework: By catching vulnerabilities early, developers spend less time on costly re-work in later stages. This frees them to focus on new feature development, increasing overall productivity.
- Accelerated Release Cycles: Integrated and automated security testing within CI/CD pipelines means security becomes a seamless part of the development process, not a last-minute bottleneck. This allows for faster, more predictable release cycles.

Example: An organization implements automated security gates in its CI/CD pipeline, reducing the average security review time from 3 days to 4 hours per release. If they have 50 releases per year, this saves hundreds of developer-days, allowing them to release features faster and capture market opportunities sooner.

- Optimized Resource Allocation: When automated tools handle routine security checks, highly skilled security analysts are freed up to focus on more complex tasks like threat intelligence, advanced penetration testing, or architectural reviews, leading to more efficient use of expertise.

4. Reduced Regulatory Fines and Legal Exposure

As detailed in Chapter 2, a growing number of regulations impose strict penalties for data breaches and non-compliance.

Proactive application security directly mitigates this financial and legal risk.

Example: A company processing credit card data that consistently fails to meet PCI DSS Requirement 6 (which focuses on secure applications) could face significant fines from payment card brands and banks, potentially losing the ability to process card transactions. A robust AppSec program ensures adherence, preventing these penalties. Similarly, failing to implement "privacy by design" in applications handling EU citizen data could lead to GDPR fines of up to €20 million or 4% of global turnover.

Summary of Cost Savings:

Source of Savings	Mechanism	Quantifiable Impact
Vulnerability Remediation	Shift-Left detection via SAST/SCA/Threat Modelling	Significant reduction in development/rework costs
Breach Prevention	Comprehensive testing, secure coding, and continuous monitoring	Avoided incident response, legal, PR, and revenue loss costs (avg. $4.88M/breach)
Operational Efficiency	CI/CD integration, automation, reduced re-work	Faster release cycles, optimized developer/security team time
Compliance & Legal	Adherence to regulations (GDPR, HIPAA, PCI DSS)	Avoided fines, legal fees, and reputational damage

Table 19

By understanding and articulating these diverse cost savings, organizations can build a compelling business case for their application security investments, demonstrating tangible financial returns rather than just presenting security as a necessary expense.

6.2 Enhanced Brand Reputation & Customer Trust

In today's digital economy, an organization's brand reputation and the trust it inspires in its customers are invaluable assets. A security breach, particularly one involving sensitive customer data, can shatter this trust overnight, leading to long-term reputational damage that far outweighs immediate financial losses. Conversely, a proactive and demonstrably secure approach to application development can significantly enhance a brand's standing and deepen customer loyalty.

1. Building and Maintaining Customer Trust

Customer trust is the bedrock of any successful business relationship. When customers interact with an application, they implicitly trust the organization to protect their personal data, financial information, and privacy. A security incident betrays this trust, leading to direct consequences:

- Customer Churn: Customers are increasingly sensitive to data privacy. Following a breach, many will switch to competitors perceived as more secure. This directly impacts revenue and market share.

Example: After a prominent social media platform experienced a large data leak due to an application vulnerability, a significant percentage of its user base migrated to alternative, privacy-focused platforms, leading to a measurable decline in active users and advertising revenue.

- Loss of Confidence: Even if a customer doesn't immediately leave, their confidence in the brand's ability to protect their information diminishes. This can impact future purchasing decisions, engagement with new services, and willingness to share additional data.

- Negative Word-of-Mouth: Dissatisfied customers are likely to share their negative experiences, amplifying the reputational damage through social media, online reviews, and traditional channels.

Conversely, a commitment to application security builds trust. When an organization can demonstrate that it prioritizes data protection, that its applications are built with security in mind, and that it has robust systems in place, customers feel safer. This fosters loyalty and encourages greater engagement. Proactive measures, such as transparent privacy policies, clear communication about security features (e.g., "our app uses end-to-end encryption"), and responsiveness to security concerns, contribute significantly to this perception.

2. Safeguarding Brand Reputation

A company's brand is its public identity and value proposition. Security incidents can inflict severe and lasting damage on this brand, affecting not just customer perception but also investor confidence, employee morale, and talent acquisition.

- Negative Media Coverage: Data breaches and security vulnerabilities are often headlining news. Negative media attention can quickly tarnish a brand's image, associating it with carelessness, incompetence, or even negligence.

- Public Scrutiny: Regulatory bodies, consumer advocacy groups, and cybersecurity experts will scrutinize an organization's security practices following a breach, often leading to public criticism and further reputational harm.

- Investor Hesitation: Investors are increasingly factoring cybersecurity risk into their investment decisions. A history of security incidents can make an organization less attractive to investors, impacting stock value and access to capital.

- Talent Attraction and Retention: Top talent, especially in technology roles, prefers to work for organizations that demonstrate a commitment to security and ethical data handling. A poor security reputation can make it harder to attract and retain skilled engineers and security professionals.

Example: A major retail brand suffered a breach where credit card information was stolen from its e-commerce application. While the immediate financial costs were significant, the long-term impact on its brand was more profound. Consumers, fearing similar incidents, shifted their online shopping to competitors. The brand spent years and millions on public relations campaigns and security overhauls to rebuild its image, a process that proved challenging and expensive.

3. Security as a Brand Differentiator

In an increasingly competitive marketplace, where many products offer similar functionalities, security can become a key differentiator. Organizations that can genuinely boast superior application security, backed by robust testing and transparent practices, can leverage this as a unique selling proposition.

- Winning New Business: For B2B companies, especially those providing SaaS solutions or handling sensitive client data, strong application security is often a mandatory requirement in procurement processes. Demonstrating a mature AppSec program can be the deciding factor in winning contracts.

- Premium Pricing: Customers in certain segments (e.g., financial services, healthcare, enterprise clients) may be willing to pay a premium for applications that offer superior security and a reduced risk profile.

- Thought Leadership: Organizations that actively share their secure development practices, contribute to open-source security projects, or participate in industry security forums can establish themselves as thought leaders, further boosting their reputation.

By consistently investing in and communicating its application security efforts, an organization transforms security from a reactive burden into a proactive force for building enduring customer trust and a resilient brand reputation.

6.3 Reduced Risk of Data Breaches & Fines

Perhaps the most direct and tangible business impact of a robust application security program is the significant reduction in the risk of data breaches and the associated financial and legal penalties. As detailed in Chapter 2, data breaches are alarmingly frequent and increasingly costly, while regulatory scrutiny continues to intensify. Proactive application security serves as the primary line of defence against these devastating outcomes.

1. Direct Reduction in Data Breach Risk

Application security testing, encompassing SAST, DAST, SCA, threat modelling, and penetration testing, is specifically designed to identify and eliminate vulnerabilities before they can be exploited by malicious actors.

- Proactive Vulnerability Removal: By finding flaws early and consistently, organizations prevent attackers from leveraging known weaknesses.

Example: A SAST tool integrated into the CI/CD pipeline prevents a critical SQL Injection vulnerability from ever reaching production. This eliminates the risk of an attacker gaining unauthorized access to the database through that specific flaw, directly preventing a potential data breach.

- Identification of Logic Flaws: Threat modelling and manual penetration testing go beyond automated checks to uncover complex business logic flaws that could lead to unauthorized access or data exfiltration.

Example: A penetration tester identifies a flaw in a payment processing application where a user can manipulate API requests to authorize transactions for a different user's account, even without their credentials. Fixing this logic flaw prevents widespread financial fraud.

- Supply Chain Security: SCA tools specifically address vulnerabilities in third-party and open-source components, which are a growing attack vector. By ensuring these dependencies are free of known critical flaws, the risk of a supply chain attack leading to a breach is significantly reduced.

The continuous nature of a mature AppSec program means that the attack surface is constantly being evaluated and hardened, making it significantly more difficult for attackers to find and exploit weaknesses. This proactive stance translates directly into a lower probability of a data breach.

2. Avoidance of Regulatory Fines and Penalties

Non-compliance with data protection regulations is no longer merely a theoretical risk; it results in substantial financial penalties and legal repercussions. A strong application security program directly supports regulatory adherence, safeguarding the organization from these punitive measures.

- General Data Protection Regulation (GDPR): GDPR mandates "data protection by design and by default" and requires organizations to implement appropriate technical and organizational measures to ensure security. Inadequate application security can lead to GDPR violations, with fines reaching up to €20 million or 4% of annual global turnover.

Example: A mobile application collects excessive user data without clear consent and stores it insecurely. A regulatory audit (triggered perhaps by a small data leak) reveals non-compliance with GDPR's data minimization and security requirements, resulting in a multi-million Euro fine. Robust AppSec practices from the design phase would have prevented this.

- Health Insurance Portability and Accountability Act (HIPAA): For healthcare organizations, HIPAA mandates strict safeguards for Protected Health Information (PHI). Application vulnerabilities that expose PHI can lead to massive fines and mandatory public breach notifications.

Example: A hospital's patient portal has a critical authentication bypass vulnerability. An attacker exploits this to access thousands of patient records. This direct HIPAA violation leads to significant fines from the Department of Health and Human Services (HHS), in addition to the reputational damage.

- Payment Card Industry Data Security Standard (PCI DSS): Companies handling credit card data must adhere to PCI DSS. Failure to maintain secure applications (Requirement 6) can result in fines imposed by payment card brands, increased transaction fees, and even the revocation of processing privileges.

Example: An e-commerce platform fails its annual PCI DSS audit due to persistent cross-site scripting (XSS) vulnerabilities in its payment pages, which could allow attackers to skim credit card data. This non-compliance leads to fines and may require the business to stop processing card payments until remediation is verified.

- Sarbanes-Oxley Act (SOX): While broader, SOX indirectly impacts application security by requiring strong internal controls over financial reporting. Insecure applications handling financial data can lead to SOX violations and hefty penalties for executive misrepresentation.

Table: Potential Penalties for AppSec Failures

Regulation/ Standard	**Example Application Security Failure**	**Potential Consequence**
GDPR	Insecure API exposes EU user PII	Fines up to €20M or 4% of global turnover **(whichever is higher),**
HIPAA	Patient portal vulnerability leads to ePHI disclosure	Significant fines, mandatory breach notifications, and corrective action plans
PCI DSS	E-commerce platform with unpatched critical web vulnerabilities	Fines from payment brands, increased transaction fees, loss of processing privileges, and potential suspension from card networks
SOX	An insecure financial reporting application susceptible to data manipulation	Legal penalties for executives, reputational damage, and investor distrust

Table 20

By proactively implementing and continuously monitoring application security controls, organizations build a strong defence against these critical business risks, protecting not only their data but also their financial stability and legal standing.

6.4 Competitive Advantage through Security Maturity

In an increasingly digitized and interconnected world, security is no longer merely a defensive measure but a strategic asset that can provide a distinct competitive advantage. Organizations that prioritize and achieve a high level of application security maturity can differentiate themselves in the marketplace, unlock new opportunities, and accelerate their pace of innovation.

1. Differentiation in the Marketplace

As security incidents become more commonplace and consumer awareness of data privacy grows, businesses and consumers are increasingly making purchasing decisions based on trust and security posture.

- Enhanced Sales and Marketing: A demonstrably secure application can be a powerful selling point. Organizations can actively market their commitment to security, leveraging certifications, positive security audit results, and a track record of no major breaches.

Example: A SaaS provider selling a CRM solution highlights its robust AppSec program, including regular penetration tests, ISO 27001 certification, and a strong DevSecOps culture. This directly influences enterprise clients who prioritize vendor security, allowing the provider to win deals against less secure competitors.

- Premium Positioning: In certain sectors, particularly those handling highly sensitive data (e.g., fintech, health tech, defence contractors), security is not just a feature; it's a prerequisite. Organizations that can confidently demonstrate superior security can command premium pricing.

- Trusted Partner Status: In a supply chain increasingly vulnerable to attacks, businesses are scrutinizing the security of their partners and suppliers. A mature AppSec program helps secure preferred vendor status and opens doors to strategic partnerships that require high security standards.

2. Unlocking New Markets and Partnerships

Regulatory landscapes and client requirements can act as barriers to entry for organizations with low security maturity. Conversely, robust application security can open up new avenues for growth.

- Entry into Regulated Industries: Compliance with stringent regulations like GDPR, HIPAA, or specific financial industry standards often requires a high level of application security. Organizations that have this embedded capability can enter and thrive in these highly lucrative, but equally highly regulated, markets.

Example: A new cloud-based payroll processing company, by investing heavily in application security from day one to achieve SOC 2 and GDPR compliance, can target large multinational corporations with strict data privacy requirements, a market inaccessible to competitors with less mature security practices.

- Strategic Alliances and Mergers/Acquisitions: Companies with a strong security posture are more attractive for strategic alliances, joint ventures, or as acquisition targets. Security debt can significantly devalue a company or make a merger problematic.

- Government Contracts: Many government contracts, especially in defense or critical infrastructure, have rigorous security requirements. A mature AppSec program is often a mandatory prerequisite for bidding on and securing such contracts.

3. Accelerated Innovation and Agility

While seemingly counterintuitive, strong application security can actually accelerate innovation and improve business agility.

- Reduced Friction in Development: By integrating security into the development pipeline from the outset (DevSecOps), security becomes a seamless part of the process, reducing late-stage bottlenecks and costly re-work. Developers can innovate faster and more confidently, knowing their code is being continuously vetted.

- "Secure by Design" Products: When security is a core design principle, applications are inherently more resilient. This frees up resources that would otherwise be spent on reactive patching or incident response, allowing teams to focus on building new features and functionalities.

- Faster Adoption of New Technologies: A security-mature organization is better equipped to evaluate and safely adopt new technologies because it has the processes, tools, and talent to understand and mitigate their associated risks.

Example: A company with a strong threat modelling culture and automated security in its CI/CD pipeline can rapidly prototype and deploy microservices-based features, knowing that potential security risks are being addressed proactively, rather than being discovered after deployment, which would slow down iteration.

Table: Security Maturity as a Competitive Advantage

Aspect of Advantage	How AppSec Maturity Delivers It	Outcome
Market Differentiation	Proactive security posture, certifications, transparent practices	Attracts security-conscious customers, enhances brand appeal, and wins competitive bids
Market Access	Compliance with stringent regulations (GDPR, HIPAA, PCI DSS)	Entry into regulated industries, global markets, and high-value client segments
Partner & Vendor Choice	Demonstrable security posture, reduced third-party risk	Preferred vendor status enables strategic alliances and smoother M&A
Innovation & Agility	Integrated DevSecOps, "secure by design" principles, rapid feedback loops	Faster time-to-market for new features, reduced development friction, safer adoption of new tech
Talent Acquisition	Reputation as a secure, responsible employer	Attracts and retains top cybersecurity and development talent

Table 21

Ultimately, achieving application security maturity shifts security from being a necessary expense to a strategic enabler. It allows organizations to operate with greater confidence, innovate more freely, and build lasting trust with their stakeholders, directly contributing to sustainable business growth and long-term success in the digital age.

Chapter 7: Conclusion

Throughout this book, we have traversed the intricate landscape of application security, moving from its fundamental business context to the strategic vision, practical implementation roadmap, and quantifiable measures of success. As we reach this concluding chapter, it is vital to synthesize the core learnings and articulate a clear path forward. Building a truly robust and resilient application security program is not a one-time project but an ongoing journey—a continuous evolution driven by an ever-changing threat landscape and the relentless pace of technological innovation.

7.1 Summary of Key Takeaways

The journey to application security maturity is complex, but the insights gained from its various facets offer a powerful blueprint for organizations striving to protect their digital assets and enhance their business value.

1. The Evolving Business Context Demands Proactive Security: Chapter 2 highlighted that the modern security landscape is characterized by a rapidly expanding attack surface, driven by widespread cloud adoption, the proliferation of microservices and APIs, and the shift to remote work. The threats themselves are becoming increasingly sophisticated, with AI-driven attacks and complex supply chain attacks posing significant challenges. Regulatory pressures from mandates like GDPR, HIPAA, and PCI DSS are intensifying, making compliance a non-negotiable aspect of doing business. Crucially, stakeholder expectations—from executives demanding risk reduction to developers seeking frictionless security—underscore the need for a holistic approach. The key takeaway here is that reactive, perimeter-based security is no longer sufficient; organizations must adopt a proactive stance, embedding security at every layer of their applications.

2. A Clear Vision and Aligned Objectives are Non-Negotiable: As explored in Chapter 3, a coherent security testing vision acts as the guiding star for all security initiatives. It defines the aspirational future state—a pervasive culture of secure software development that protects customers, safeguards data, and fuels innovation with trust. Translating this vision into concrete, SMART (Specific, Measurable, Achievable, Relevant, Time-bound) or OKR-based long-term objectives is essential for strategic planning. These objectives, spanning risk reduction, operational efficiency, cultural development, and compliance, ensure that security efforts are focused and measurable. The main principle is the deep alignment of application security goals with broader business objectives, transforming security from a perceived cost centre into a recognized business enabler. When security speaks the language of risk, revenue, and reputation, it gains the necessary buy-in and resources.

3. A Phased Roadmap for Practical Implementation is Essential: Chapter 4 detailed a pragmatic, three-phase roadmap for building and maturing an application security program.

- **Phase 1: Foundation** emphasizes establishing security testing basics, including understanding and implementing SAST, DAST, SCA, and manual reviews. This phase also focuses on selecting and strategically implementing tools that fit the organization's unique context, and crucially, building a foundational security-aware culture through leadership buy-in and security champion programs. An initial risk assessment and the definition of baseline metrics provide the starting point for measuring progress.

- **Phase 2: Integration** drives the "shift-left" philosophy, embedding security activities into every stage of the SDLC (DevSecOps). This involves defining security requirements in planning, conducting threat modelling in design, integrating security tools directly into developer workflows (e.g., in-IDE SAST), implementing security-focused code reviews, and ensuring continuous testing in CI/CD pipelines. Developer training on secure coding practices becomes paramount, making them the first line of defence.

- **Phase 3: Automation & Scale** elevates the program to an enterprise level. This involves advanced automation of security testing through orchestration platforms, intelligent false positive reduction, and policy-as-code for consistent enforcement. Leveraging AI and Machine Learning for enhanced threat detection and intelligent prioritization becomes a strategic advantage. Scaling security across a vast application portfolio requires centralized governance with decentralized execution, strong ASPM solutions, and robust supply chain security management. Throughout all phases, the emphasis remains on continuous improvement and feedback loops, ensuring adaptability to new threats and technologies.

4. Metrics are the Language of Success and Value: Chapter 5 underscored that "what gets measured gets managed." Quantifiable metrics are indispensable for proving the effectiveness of the application security program and demonstrating its value to the business.

- **Vulnerability Detection & Remediation Rates** show how effectively flaws are found and fixed, impacting the overall security debt.

- **Mean Time to Detect (MTTD) is a** critical time-based metric that reflects the agility and efficiency of security testing, directly influencing the exposure window and potential impact of incidents.

- **Test Coverage & Compliance Adherence** ensure the comprehensiveness of security efforts and confirm adherence to legal and regulatory obligations.
- **Return on Investment (ROI) of Security Testing Initiatives** translates technical achievements into tangible financial benefits, such as avoided breach costs, reduced remediation expenses, and increased operational efficiencies. These metrics are crucial for justifying ongoing investment and illustrating security as a strategic asset.

5. Application Security Drives Tangible Business Impact: Finally, Chapter 6 brought into sharp focus the profound business impact of a mature application security program.

- **Cost Savings from Proactive Security** are realized through reduced remediation expenses by "shifting left," avoiding the astronomical costs of data breaches (average $4.88 million), increased operational efficiency, and faster development cycles due to fewer security bottlenecks.
- **Enhanced Brand Reputation & Customer Trust** are invaluable assets that are protected and strengthened by a demonstrable commitment to security. Avoiding breaches and maintaining data privacy builds loyalty and differentiates the organization in the marketplace.
- **Reduced Risk of Data Breaches & Fines** is a direct outcome, mitigating the threat of severe financial penalties (e.g., GDPR fines up to €20 million) and legal repercussions.
- **Competitive Advantage through Security Maturity** transforms security into a unique selling proposition, enabling entry into new, highly regulated markets, securing strategic partnerships, and attracting top talent. It allows

organizations to innovate with confidence and agility, leading to sustainable growth.

In essence, the key takeaway is clear: application security is no longer merely a technical checklist or a departmental silo. It is a strategic imperative that, when approached systematically and with a business-aligned vision, fundamentally contributes to an organization's financial health, market position, and long-term viability.

7.2 Next Steps for the Organization's Security Journey

The completion of a roadmap, or even the achievement of initial objectives, is merely a pause in the continuous journey of application security. To maintain a robust and adaptive security posture, organizations must commit to ongoing evolution and strategic refinement. Here are the crucial next steps for any organization looking to sustain and advance its application security maturity:

1. Sustain and Mature Foundational Practices: The basics, once established, must be rigorously maintained and continuously improved. This means:

- **Regular Tool Tuning:** Continuously refine SAST, DAST, and SCA tool configurations to reduce false positives and enhance accuracy. This iterative process is vital to maintain developer trust and efficiency.
- **Ongoing Cultural Reinforcement:** The security-aware culture needs constant nourishment. This includes regular, fresh, and engaging developer training, promoting the security champions program, and consistently celebrating secure development practices. Regular check-ins on psychological safety within teams will ensure open communication about security concerns.

- **Baseline Evolution:** The initial risk assessment and baseline metrics established in Phase 1 should not be static. They must be revisited regularly, adapting to new business lines, evolving threats, and changes in the application portfolio. This ensures that the organization is always measuring what truly matters and focusing on the most critical risks.

2. Deepen Automation and AI/ML Integration: Building on Phase 3, the next steps involve expanding the reach and intelligence of automation:

- **End-to-End Orchestration:** Move towards a fully integrated AppSec platform that orchestrates all security tools, centralizing data, and automating workflows from code commit to production monitoring. This reduces manual intervention and provides real-time holistic visibility.
- **Advanced Predictive Analytics:** Further leverage AI/ML to move beyond anomaly detection to predictive security. This includes using machine learning to identify code patterns likely to introduce vulnerabilities, predict potential attack paths, and dynamically adjust security controls based on observed real-time threat intelligence.
- **Automated Remediation Expansion (with Guardrails):** Explore opportunities for increasingly automated remediation of low-risk, common vulnerabilities, potentially through auto-generating pull requests for dependency updates or configuration fixes, always with human oversight and clear approval workflows. This will significantly reduce the manual burden of security debt.

3. Embrace Proactive Security by Default: Security must become an inherent characteristic of all applications, rather than an add-on.

- **Mandatory Threat Modelling:** Implement threat modelling as a mandatory step for all new application development, major feature additions, and significant architectural changes. This ensures that security is considered at the earliest design stages.

- **Secure Design Principles as Standard:** Integrate secure design patterns and architectural principles into the organization's standard operating procedures. This promotes "security by default" in how applications are conceptualized.

- **Security Requirements as First-Class Citizens:** Elevate security requirements to the same level of importance as functional requirements from the project initiation phase, ensuring they are well-defined, testable, and prioritized.

4. Prioritize Continuous Learning and Adaptation: The cybersecurity landscape is in constant evolution. Organizations must be agile and responsive.

- **Robust Threat Intelligence Integration:** Establish strong channels for consuming and acting upon real-time threat intelligence. This includes subscribing to industry alerts, participating in information-sharing communities, and integrating threat feeds into security operations.

- **Regular Program Review:** Conduct annual or bi-annual comprehensive reviews of the entire application security program. Assess its effectiveness against established objectives, identify emerging gaps, and recalibrate strategy based on lessons learned from internal incidents and external threat intelligence.

- **Cross-Pollination of Knowledge:** Foster continuous learning across teams through workshops, internal conferences, and knowledge-sharing sessions. Encourage developers to attend security conferences and bring back new insights.

5. **Strengthen Cross-Functional Collaboration and Accountability:** The "shared responsibility" model needs continuous nurturing.

- **Formalized DevSecOps Frameworks:** Continuously mature the DevSecOps framework, ensuring clear roles, responsibilities, and accountability for security outcomes across development, operations, and security teams.
- **Business Unit Engagement:** Maintain open lines of communication with business unit leaders, ensuring they understand the business value of security and are actively involved in risk prioritization for their applications.
- **Transparent Reporting to Leadership:** Provide clear, concise, and business-oriented reports on the security posture and ROI of security investments to the executive leadership and board. This ensures continued strategic alignment and resource allocation.

By committing to these next steps, an organization can move beyond merely "having" an application security program to truly "being" a secure and resilient entity, capable of navigating the complexities of the digital age with confidence.

7.3 Call to Action: Building a Secure Future

The digital transformation sweeping across industries offers unprecedented opportunities for innovation, growth, and global connectivity. Yet, with every technological leap comes an accompanying rise in sophisticated cyber threats, making the security of our applications paramount. The insights and strategies presented in this book are not merely academic exercises; they are a call to action.

Building a secure future for any organization is not the sole responsibility of a dedicated security team; it is a collective imperative. Every developer, every architect, every product manager, every operations engineer, and indeed, every leader, plays a vital role. It demands a fundamental shift in mindset: from security as a reactive bottleneck to security as a proactive, integrated enabler of business value.

The journey to application security maturity is challenging, requiring sustained commitment, continuous learning, and strategic investment. There will be setbacks, new vulnerabilities will emerge, and the adversaries will adapt. However, the costs of inaction—the devastating impact of data breaches, the erosion of customer trust, the burden of regulatory fines, and the loss of competitive edge—far outweigh the efforts required to build robust application security.

Therefore, the call to action is clear and resonant:

- **For Leadership:** Champion application security as a strategic business initiative. Invest in the right tools, talent, and training. Foster a culture of security from the top down. Understand and demand metrics that demonstrate value, not just compliance.

- **For Development Teams:** Embrace secure coding practices as a core skill. Integrate security tools into your daily workflows. Actively participate in threat modelling. Become security champions within your teams. View security as an integral part of delivering high-quality, trusted software.

- **For Security Professionals:** Be strategic partners to the business. Speak the language of risk and value. Facilitate, enable, and empower development teams. Continually learn and adapt to the evolving threat landscape.

- **For Everyone:** Recognize that security is a shared responsibility. Every decision, every line of code, every deployment choice has security implications. Be vigilant, be curious, and be proactive.

The future of digital business belongs to those who can build trust and resilience into their very foundation. By committing to the vision of secure software development, embracing the roadmap for continuous improvement, and acting collectively, any organization can not only protect itself from the threats of today but also lay the groundwork for a more secure, innovative, and prosperous tomorrow. Let us build this secure future, together.

30/60/90 DAY ACTION PLAN

Based on the book's three-phase approach, here's a practical implementation plan sample:

30-DAY SPRINT: FOUNDATION QUICKSTART

Week 1: Assessment & Buy-in

Day 1-2: Executive briefing using Chapter 6 ROI data

- Present average breach cost

- Show shift-left savings

- Get formal sponsorship

Day 3-5: Form Core AppSec Team

- Identify security champion candidates (1 per dev team)

- Assign a dedicated AppSec lead

- Schedule kick-off meeting

Week 2: Current State Analysis

Day 6-8: Application Inventory (Chapter 4.4 template)

- List all applications
- Classify by criticality to business (Critical/High/Medium/Low)
- Identify the top 3 critical applications to the business

- *Day 9-10: Baseline Metrics Collection*

  - Run SAST on one critical application
  - Document current vulnerabilities
  - Calculate initial vulnerability density

Week 3: Tool Selection & Pilot

Day 11-15: Tool Evaluation (Chapter 4.2 criteria)

- SAST: Evaluate 2-3 options
- SCA: Test on current dependencies
- Secret Scanner: Immediate implementation
- Select based on: Language support, IDE integration, False positive rate

Week 4: Initial Implementation

Day 16-20: Pilot Program Launch

- Implement SAST in one team's CI/CD
- Run the first security training session
- Create first threat model (1 critical app)

Day 21-30: Foundation Establishment

- Document secure coding guidelines
- Set up vulnerability tracking in Jira/similar
- Establish weekly security sync meetings

30-Day Success Metrics:

- ✓ Executive sponsorship secured
- ✓ Baseline metrics established
- ✓ 1+ security tool implemented
- ✓ First threat model completed

60-DAY EXPANSION: INTEGRATION PHASE

Month 2, Week 1-2: Developer Enablement

Day 31-35: Comprehensive Training Rollout

- OWASP Top 10 training for all developers
- Language-specific secure coding (Java/Python/JS)
- Hands-on remediation workshops

Day 36-40: IDE Integration

- Install SAST plugins in all developer IDEs
- Configure pre-commit hooks
- Create remediation quick-reference guides

Month 2, Week 3-4: Process Integration

Day 41-45: SDLC Integration (Chapter 4.5)

- Add security requirements to story templates
- Integrate SAST/SCA into all CI/CD pipelines
- Define security gates (no high/critical to production)

Day 46-50: Expand Coverage

- Add DAST for staging environments
- Implement dependency checking (SCA)
- Start weekly vulnerability review meetings

Month 2, Week 5-6: Cultural Development

Day 51-55: Security Champions Program

- Formally appoint champions
- Provide advanced training
- Create an internal security Slack channel

Day 56-60: Governance Framework

- Publish security policies
- Create an exception handling process
- Define SLAs for vulnerability remediation

60-Day Success Metrics:

- ✓ 50%+ developers trained
- ✓ Security tools in 75%+ pipelines
- ✓ Security champions active
- ✓ 30% reduction in new vulnerabilities

90-DAY MATURATION: EARLY AUTOMATION

Month 3, Week 1-2: Advanced Tooling

Day 61-65: Orchestration Setup

- Implement ASPM or build a dashboard
- Automate vulnerability aggregation
- Create executive reporting

Day 66-70: Advanced Testing

- Schedule the first penetration test
- Implement IAST for complex apps
- Add container scanning

Month 3, Week 3-4: Optimization

Day 71-75: Noise Reduction

- Tune tools to reduce false positives
- Create baseline suppressions
- Implement smart triage rules

Day 76-80: Automation Expansion

- Auto-create tickets for high/critical
- Implement auto-remediation for dependencies
- Add security regression tests

Month 3, Week 5-6: Measurement & Planning

Day 81-85: Metrics Review

- Calculate ROI of initiatives

- Measure MTTD

- Document cost savings

Day 86-90: Future Roadmap

- Plan Phase 3 automation

- Budget for next year

- Create 12-month maturity roadmap

90-Day Success Metrics:

- ✓ 100% critical apps covered

- ✓ MTTR < 30 days for critical

- ✓ Demonstrated ROI

- ✓ Year 2 roadmap approved

SUCCESS CRITERIA CHECKLIST

Technical Implementation Success

Tools & Technology

- [ ] SAST is integrated in 100% of repositories
- [ ] SCA scanning on all dependencies daily
- [ ] SBOM generation
- [ ] DAST running on all external-facing apps
- [ ] Secret scanning in pre-commit hook
- [ ] Security gates blocking critical vulnerabilities

Process Integration

- [ ] Security requirements in every user story
- [ ] Threat modelling for new features
- [ ] Automated vulnerability tracking
- [ ] Clear remediation SLAs are defined and met
- [ ] Regular penetration testing is scheduled

Cultural Transformation Success

Training & Awareness

- [ ] 90%+ developers completed security training
- [ ] Security champions in every team
- [ ] Monthly security awareness communications
- [ ] Positive developer feedback on tools
- [ ] Security is considered in architecture decisions

Collaboration Metrics

- [ ] Weekly security/dev sync meetings
- [ ] < 2-day response time on security questions
- [ ] Developers proactively consulting security
- [ ] Security backlog is actively prioritized
- [ ] Cross-team security knowledge sharing

Business Impact Success

Risk Reduction

- ☐ 50%+ reduction in critical vulnerabilities
- ☐ 0 security breaches from known vulnerabilities
- ☐ 75%+ reduction in production security issues
- ☐ Compliance audit findings decreased

Financial Returns

- ☐ Shift-left savings documented
- ☐ Avoided breach costs calculated
- ☐ Reduced emergency patch costs
- ☐ Lower cyber insurance premiums
- ☐ Faster feature delivery (no security delays)

Strategic Outcomes

- ☐ Security as a differentiator in sales
- ☐ Passed customer security assessments
- ☐ Board-level security metrics reporting
- ☐ Security roadmap funded for next year
- ☐ Industry recognition for security practices

Continuous Improvement Indicators

- ☐ Monthly metrics showing positive trends
- ☐ Regular tool and process optimization
- ☐ Proactive adoption of new security practices
- ☐ Lessons learned, documented and applied
- ☐ Security program maturity assessment improved

Red Flags to Watch

- ☐ Increasing vulnerability backlog
- ☐ Developer complaints about friction
- ☐ Security tools are frequently bypassed
- ☐ Metrics manipulation instead of improvement
- ☐ The security team becoming a bottleneck

This comprehensive action plan and success criteria provide readers with a concrete path forward, transforming the book's concepts into actionable steps with measurable outcomes.

List of Abbreviations

S. No	Abbreviation	Full Form
1	SCA	Software Composition Analysis
2	SAST	Static Application Security Testing
3	DAST	Dynamic Application Security Testing
4	IAST	Interactive Application Security Testing
5	RASP	Runtime Application Self-Protection
6	DevOps	Development Operations
7	DevSecOps	Development Security Operations
8	SecOps	Security Operations
9	API	Application Programming Interface
10	APP	Application
11	GDPR	General Data Protection Regulation
12	HIPAA	Health Insurance Portability and Accountability Act
13	PCI DSS	Payment Card Industry Data Security Standard
14	NIST	National Institute of Standards and Technology
15	CSA	Cloud Security Alliance
16	SOX	Sarbanes-Oxley Act
17	SOC	Service Organization Control
18	SDLC	Software Development Live Cycle
19	SSDLC	Secure Software Development Live Cycle
20	CI/CD	Continuous Integration/Continuous Deployment
21	AppSec	Application Security
22	Pen Testing	Penetration Testing
23	CEO	Chief Executive Officer
24	CTO	Chief Technology Officer
25	CIO	Chief Information Officer
26	CISO	Chief Information Security Officer
27	MTTD	Mean Time to Detect
28	ROI	Return on Investment
29	IAC	Infrastructure as Code
30	YoY	Year on Year

S. No	Abbreviation	Full Form
31	SMBs	Small and Medium-sized Businesses
32	IBM	International Business Machines
33	OSS	Open Source Software
34	GenAI	Generative Artificial Intelligence
35	AI	Artificial Intelligence
36	EU	European Union
37	WAF	Web Application Firewall
38	FW	Firewall
39	ISO/IEC	International Organization of Standardization/ International Electrotechnical Commission
40	CSF	Cybersecurity Framework
41	SaaS	Software as a Service
42	ISMS	Information Security Management Systems
43	Vuln Management	Vulnerability Management
44	QA	Quality Assurance
45	XSS	Cross-Site Scripting
46	IDOR	Insecure Direct Object Reference
47	SMART	Specific Measurable Achievable Relevant Time Bound
48	OKR	Objective Key Result
49	DFD	Data Flow Diagram
50	IDE	Integrated Development Environment
51	NVD	National Vulnerability Database
52	AST	Application Security Testing
53	SCM	Software Configuration Management
54	OWASP	Open Web Application Security Project
55	MVS	Minimum Viable Security
56	CTF	Capture the Flag
57	PTO	Personal Time Off
58	KPI	Key Performance Indicator
59	PII	Personal Identifiable Information
60	PHI	Protected Health Information
61	IDS	Intrusion Detection Systems

S. No	Abbreviation	Full Form
62	IPS	Intrusion Prevention Systems
63	LoC	Lines of Code
64	TTR	Time to Remediate
65	MTTR	Mean Time to Remediate
66	Q, Q1	Quarter, Quarter 1
67	STRIDE	Spoofing Tampering Repudiation Information Disclosure Denial of Service Elevation of Privilege
68	DREAD	Damage Potential Reproducibility Exploitability Affected Users Discoverability
69	PASTA	Process for Attack Simulation and Threat Analysis
70	CVSS	Common Vulnerability Scoring System
71	CVE	Common Vulnerabilities and Exposures
72	AI/ML	Artificial Intelligence/Machine Learning
73	ASPM	Application Security Posture Management
74	KLoC	Kilo Line of Code
75	TPR	True Positive Rate
76	FPR	False Positive Rate
77	SBOM	Software Bill of Materials

List of Tables

List of Figures

References

S. No	Link	Status	Result
1	https://www.cisa.gov/resources-tools/resources/cybersecurity-best-practices-guidance	Page Not Found	https://www.cisa.gov/topics/cybersecurity-best-practices
2	https://www.edps.europa.eu/data-protection/our-work/subjects/general-data-protection-regulation_en	Working	
3	https://www.ibm.com/downloads/cas/M0MEY7J4	Page Not Found	https://www.ibm.com/downloads/documents/us-en/107a02e94948f4ec
4	https://learn.microsoft.com/en-us/security/benchmark/azure/security-controls-v3-security-best-practices-overview	Page Not Found	https://learn.microsoft.com/en-us/security/benchmark/azure/overview-v3
5	https://www.nist.gov/cyberframework	Page Not Found	The NIST Cybersecurity Framework (CSF) 2.0
6	https://owasp.org/www-project-top-10/	Page Not Found	https://owasp.org/www-project-top-ten/
7	https://owasp.org/www-project-top-10-for-large-language-model-applications/assets/PDF/OWASP-Top-10-for-LLMs-v2025.pdf	Working	
8	https://www.pcisecuritystandards.org/	Working	
9	https://www.hhs.gov/hipaa/for-professionals/index.html	Working	
10	https://www.verizon.com/business/resources/Tea/reports/2025-dbir-data-breach-investigations-report.pdf	Working	

Made in United States
Troutdale, OR
11/03/2026

56845274R00106